The History of the Dress of the Royal Regiment of Artillery,

1625–1897.

THE DRUM MAJOR OF THE ROYAL REGIMENT OF ARTILLERY.
Circa 1840.

THE HISTORY OF THE DRESS

OF THE

ROYAL REGIMENT OF ARTILLERY,

1625–1897.

Compiled and Illustrated by

CAPTAIN R. J. MACDONALD, R.A.

The Naval & Military Press Ltd

Published by

The Naval & Military Press Ltd
Unit 10 Ridgewood Industrial Park,
Uckfield, East Sussex,
TN22 5QE England

Tel: +44 (0) 1825 749494
Fax: +44 (0) 1825 765701

www.naval-military-press.com
www.military-genealogy.com

*In reprinting in facsimile from the original, any imperfections are inevitably reproduced
and the quality may fall short of modern type and cartographic standards.*

TO

HIS ROYAL HIGHNESS

FIELD-MARSHAL THE DUKE OF CAMBRIDGE,

K.G., K.T., K.P., G.C.B., G.C.S.I., G.C.M.G.,

COLONEL-IN-CHIEF OF THE ROYAL REGIMENT OF ARTILLERY,

THIS

HISTORY OF ITS DRESS

IS RESPECTFULLY AND BY PERMISSION

DEDICATED

BY

THE AUTHOR.

The Edition of this work has been strictly limited as follows:—

300 *Copies for Guarantors, being First Proofs.*

700 *Copies for Subscribers before publication.*

500 *Copies for Sale.*

On completion of which the plates were destroyed.

Guarantor's Copy. No **51.**

(*Signature*) Reginald T. Hardwick
Capt., R.A.

PREFACE.

IN placing this work before my brother Officers, and others interested in military dress from an historical point of view, I beg to ask that any who may read it will not be too severe in their criticisms, either from a literary or from an artistic point of view. This being my first effort, I send it out for perusal with a hope that it may meet with the approval of all who are interested in the subject.

When I first joined the Regiment, in 1887, it was my ambition to obtain all original prints, books, drawings, and MSS. dealing with the costume of the Royal Artillery; and I now have in my possession a complete collection of the above, from which this work is compiled. It was at the request of the Committee of the Royal Artillery Institution that I undertook to paint a series of water-colour sketches illustrative of the dress of the Regiment.

This work is written as a supplement to Kane's "List of Officers of the Royal Regiment of Artillery," and it is through the kind help of the Committee of the Royal Artillery Institution I am now able to produce in book-form the results of my study. Several histories of the Royal Artillery have been written, but up to the present time none have been illustrated. My drawings will be of value more on account of their aim at accuracy of detail than for their artistic merit. I have carried out the scheme of dividing the work into chapters, each corresponding to a separate reign. This, as will be seen at a glance, makes some of the chapters very much longer than others, and such, of course, contain many more drawings: George III. and Queen Victoria's

PREFACE.

reigns in particular absorb a great many of the illustrations, and much of the letterpress. This, however, could not be avoided.

In designing a plate, I have always endeavoured to go on the principle of having two independent authorities to vouch for it. I have obtained the information first from a portrait or print, and then verified it by means of any orders for dress or MSS., etc., dealing with the date in question.

Before concluding, I wish to express the great obligation I am under to the present Secretary of the Royal Artillery Institution, for his very great assistance to me in the production of this history.

WOOLWICH,
September 30th, 1898.

CONTENTS.

	PAGE
INTRODUCTION	1
REIGN OF CHARLES I.	3
THE COMMONWEALTH	6
CHARLES II.	7
JAMES II.	11
WILLIAM AND MARY	15
ANNE	19
GEORGE I.	21
GEORGE II.	22
GEORGE III.	29
GEORGE IV.	75
WILLIAM IV.	81
VICTORIA	93

PLATE SECTION

LIST OF COLOURED PLATES.

FRONTISPIECE.—Drum-Major of the Royal Regiment of Artillery ... ... circa 1840

PLATE No. 1. Train of Artillery 1660–1702

2. Train of Artillery 1702–1714

3. Royal Artillery 1743

4. Royal Artillery 1760

5. Royal Artillery 1764

6. Royal Artillery 1778

7. Royal Horse Artillery 1793

8. Royal Artillery 1794

9. Royal Artillery 1797

10. Royal Artillery 1799

11. Royal Horse Artillery 1815

12. Royal Horse Artillery (Rocket Troop) 1815

13. Royal Artillery 1815

14. Royal Artillery 1820

15. Royal Horse Artillery 1823

16. Royal Horse Artillery 1828

17. Royal Artillery 1828

18. Royal Artillery 1840

19. Royal Horse Artillery 1850

20. Royal Artillery 1854

21. Royal Horse Artillery 1855

22. Royal Artillery 1864

23. Royal Horse Artillery 1893

24. Royal Artillery 1897

TRAIN OF ARTILLERY
1660-1702.

TRAIN OF ARTILLERY.

1702-1714.

ROYAL ARTILLERY.
1743.

ROYAL ARTILLERY.
1760.

ROYAL ARTILLERY.
1764.

ROYAL ARTILLERY.
1778.

ROYAL HORSE ARTILLERY.

1793.

ROYAL ARTILLERY.

1794.

ROYAL ARTILLERY.

1797.

ROYAL ARTILLERY.

1799.

ROYAL HORSE ARTILLERY.
1815.

ROYAL HORSE ARTILLERY.
Rocket Troop.
1815.

ROYAL ARTILLERY.

1815.

ROYAL ARTILLERY.

1820.

ROYAL HORSE ARTILLERY.
1823.

ROYAL HORSE ARTILLERY.
1828.

ROYAL ARTILLERY.
1828.

ROYAL ARTILLERY.

1840.

ROYAL HORSE ARTILLERY.
1850.

ROYAL ARTILLERY.

1854.

ROYAL HORSE ARTILLERY.
1855.

ROYAL ARTILLERY.

1864.

ROYAL HORSE ARTILLERY.
1893.

ROYAL ARTILLERY.

1897.

SUMMARY OF AUTHORITIES.

PRINTS, PORTRAITS, ETC.

Description.	Title.	Date.	Drawn by	Published by
Coloured engraving	Master-Gunner Eldred, "The Gunner's Glasse"	1642		
Painting	Portrait of General Borgard, R.A.	circa 1710		
Painting	Portrait of Colonel Jonas Watson, R.A.	circa 1710		
Coloured litho	Portrait of Captain John Romer, Engineer	1710	—	Porter's "Hist. of R.E."
Two water-colour sketches	The "Cloathing of H.M. Forces"	1743		
Engraving	Portrait of Captain Tiffin, R.A.	circa 1759		
Painting	Portrait of Colonel Griffith Williams, R.A.	circa 1760		
Painting	Portrait of Thomas Hosmer, R.A.	1760		
Painting	Portrait of Captain John Goodwin, R.A.	circa 1764	Sir W. Beechey	
Miniature	Portrait of an Officer R.A. (no name)	circa 1764		
Pencil sketch	An Officer in camp at Warley	1778		
Painting	Portrait of Captain Patterson, R.A.	circa 1778		
Miniature	Portrait of an Officer (no name)	circa 1778		
Painting	Portrait of Colonel Stehelin, R.A.	circa 1780		
Coloured print	The Artillery Driver	1792		
Miniature	Portrait of an Officer R.H.A.	circa 1793		
Water-colour sketch	In Captain Lawson's "Evolutions of R.H.A." MS. notes	1793		
Painting	Portrait of Captain Scott, R.A.	circa 1793		
Coloured print	Sadler's Flying Artillery	1798	Sadler	Rowlandson
Coloured print	Present arms—First Motion (an Artillery sentry)	1797	Scott	Scott
Miniature	Portrait of an Officer R.A. (no name)	circa 1797		
Painting	Portrait of Lieut.-General Congreve, R.A.	circa 1797		
Coloured print	From the "British Military Library"	1799		
Water-colour sketches	From "Experiments in Artillery Movements." MSS.	1799		
Coloured print	The French Invasion	1803	—	Humphreys

SUMMARY OF AUTHORITIES.

Description.	Title.	Date.	Drawn by	Published by
Two coloured prints	From Atkinson's "Picturesque Costume of Great Britain"	1806	T. A. Atkinson	W. Miller
Two coloured prints	From Goddard's "Armies of Europe"	1812	—	T. Goddard
Two coloured prints	Artilleur Anglaise	circa 1812	C. Vernet	
Coloured print	No title (Driver of Artillery)	circa 1812		
Painting	Portrait of Colonel Percy Drummond	circa 1812		
Coloured print	From the "Picturesque Representation of the Dress and Manners of the English"	1814	—	J. Murray
Three coloured prints	From "History of the King's German Legion," by Beamish	1814		
Coloured print	From Congreve's "Rocket System"	1814		
Engraving	From Booth's "History of the Battle of Waterloo"	1815	Geo. Johnes	Booth
Three coloured prints	From "The Military Costume of the British Empire"	1815	C. H. Smith	
Coloured print	R.A. Barracks, Woolwich	1816	Cockburn	Colnaghi
Sketch	The Garrison Staff, Woolwich, in 1820	1820		
Coloured print	The Rotunda, Woolwich	1820	Lucas	Lucas
Coloured print	Officer R.H.A.	1820	W. Heath	J. Watson
Three coloured prints	Officers R.H.A. and R.A., and Gunner R.A.	1828	E. Hull	Engelman
Three coloured prints	From *Gentleman's Magazine of Fashion*	1828–32		
Coloured print	No title (Driver Corps)	1829	Alken	S. Fuller
Coloured print	Woolwich	1829	Eug. Lami	Colnaghi
Three coloured prints	Officers R.H.A. and R.A.	circa 1829	Heath	Heath
Coloured print	Officer R.A.	1829	Alken	Ackermann
Print	Artillerie Anglaise	circa 1830	Moltzheim	
Four coloured prints	R.H.A., Rocket Troop and R.A.	1831	Heath	Colnaghi
Four coloured prints	R.H.A. and R.A.	circa 1831	C. H. Martin	Spooner
Water-colour sketch	Gun Team R.A.	1835		
Painting	Officer R.H.A.	1833	Drusheme	
Coloured print	The Drum-Major of the Royal Artillery	circa 1840	A. Comer, 1st Dragoon Guards	E. Jones
Water-colour	Trumpeter of the R.A.	circa 1840	W. Heath	
Two coloured prints	R.H.A. in Action: Guard-mounting	1840	M. A. Hayes	Ackermann

SUMMARY OF AUTHORITIES.

Description.	Title.	Date.	Drawn by	Published by
Coloured print	Royal Artillery, No. 2	1840	Heath	Ackermann
Coloured print	Officer R.H.A.	1842	Giles	Ackermann
Three coloured prints	R.H.A., R.A. Repository Exercises: Rocket Practice in the Marshes.	1843–45	Jones	Grant
Coloured print	Royal Foot Artillery	1846	Martens	Ackermann
Two coloured prints	R.H.A. and R.A.	1846	M. A. Hayes	H. Graves
Coloured print	Officer R.H.A.	1849	Martens	Ackermann
Six coloured prints	R.H.A., R.A., Mountain and Siege Artillery	1850	Campion	Ackermann
Two coloured prints	R.H.A. and R.A.	1853	Martens	Ackermann
Coloured print	Officer R.H.A.	1854	Campion	Ackermann
Two coloured prints	R.H.A. and R.A.	1855	—	E. Gambart
Coloured print	Officers R.A.	1855	Martens	Ackermann
Coloured print	R.H.A., Field Artillery, and Garrison Artillery	1861	G. Thomas	Day & Son
Coloured print	The Royal Artillery	1856	Sharpe	Gambart
	From 1860 to 1897, photographs form the principal authorities			
	Two books of photographs in the R.A.I., about 1860–1870			
	Present-day studies made from life and photographs			

WORKS CONSULTED.

Planché's "History of British Costume."

"The History of Dress from the Earliest Period till the Close of the Eighteenth Century." By F. W. Fairholt, F.S.A.

"A Critical Inquiry into Ancient Armour as it existed in Europe, but particularly in England, from the Norman Conquest to the Reign of Charles II." By Sir S. Meyrick.

"The History of the British Army." By Grose.

"History of the King's German Legion." By Beamish.

"The History of the Dress of the British Soldier." By Luard.

The *Gentleman's Magazine of Fashion.* 1828–32.

SUMMARY OF AUTHORITIES.

Experiments in Artillery. MS. Notes. 1799.
MS. Notes by the late General Mercer.
Cleaveland's "Notes on the Early History of the R.A."
Duncan's "History of the R.A."
Kane's List. Notes on Dress.
"History of the British Standing Army, A.D. 1660–1700." By Colonel Clifford Walton, C.B.
Dress Regulations from earliest to present date.
The "British Military Library. 1799."

DRESS REGULATIONS CONSULTED.

1825. Regulations for the Provision of Clothing, etc., for the Royal Regiment of Artillery.
1833. Regulations for the Dress and Appointments of General, Staff, and Regimental Officers, and the Non-commissioned Officers and Men of the Royal Regiment of Artillery.
1855. Regulations for the Dress and Appointments of General, Staff, and Regimental Officers, and the Non-commissioned Officers and Men of the Royal Regiment of Artillery.
1864. Standing Orders, Dress Regulations, and Trumpet and Bugle sounds for the Royal Regiment of Artillery.
1874. Dress Regulations for the Army.
1876. Standing Orders of the Royal Regiment of Artillery.
1883. Dress Regulations for the Army.
1891. Ditto ditto.
1894. Ditto ditto.

UNIFORMS, ETC.

Officer's Full-dress Coatee. 1812–15.
R.H.A. Helmet, worn by Lieut.-Gen. Webber Smith, R.A., through the Peninsular War. 1809.
R.H.A. Jacket. 1835.
Coatee, Chako, Breastplate, Sword, worn by R.A. Officer. 1854.
Pelisse, Busby, Barrelled Sash, worn by R.H.A. Officer. 1854.
R.H.A. Jacket. 1854.

INTRODUCTION BY SECRETARY R.A.I.

ABOUT twelve years ago, an attempt was made to obtain a series of coloured plates of Royal Artillery uniform. The Committee of the Royal Artillery Institution obtained the names of certain Officers willing to guarantee the expenses of production; these were not sufficient, and the project lapsed, but the original list of guarantors remains as the foundation of that now published.

The author of "The History of the Dress of the Royal Artillery," while serving at Woolwich shortly after joining the Regiment, noted the failure to produce the plates, and set to work to study the history of the regimental dress.

The Committee of the Institution recognized, about the year 1892, that in him there seemed a probability of finding one who would be capable of doing justice to the plates of regimental uniform; they granted leave to their Secretary to try and arrange with him the best means of publishing a series of plates or a book on the subject.

To this end another and successful effort was made to obtain guarantees. As soon as this was done, a subscription form was sent to every Colonel, Lieutenant-Colonel, and Major in the Regiment, asking them to find out which of the Officers under their respective commands wished to subscribe for a copy; the result appears in the list of guarantors and subscribers, which shows that the complete edition of 1000 copies is exhausted by subscription; another result is that all fear of a call upon the guarantors soon disappeared, and instead, each guarantor now receives a signed first-proof copy at the same price as a subscriber receives his copy.

As soon as the financial difficulties began to disappear, the Committee sanctioned the obtaining of estimates and specimen plates from various firms. It was only after many months of careful inquiries and trials that the employment of the French firm of Goupil et C$^{ie.}$ to produce the coloured plates was agreed upon, and the Committee feel that they have no cause to regret the decision.

Throughout the whole of the inquiries most valuable advice has been given by Mr. John Murray, of 50, Albemarle Street, W., and to him the Committee and Author tender their best thanks.

In conclusion, the Committee wish it to be known that they regard this book as a supplement to Kane's "List of Officers of the Royal Artillery;" they feel that a student of regimental history, letters, or biography will find his studies greatly enlightened by references to "Kane's List" and this book, and that by helping in the publication of these works they are carrying out to a very high degree the ideas of the founders of the Royal Artillery Institution.

A. J. ABDY, Major,

Secretary R.A.I.

Woolwich,
October, 1898.

THE HISTORY OF THE DRESS OF THE ROYAL REGIMENT OF ARTILLERY.

INTRODUCTION.

THE period selected to commence this history is the reign of Charles I., as it was about this date that armour was going out of fashion. The introduction of firearms had materially assisted in bringing about this modification, though cuirasses and gorgets were still worn as late as the reign of Queen Anne.

James I. is stated to have remarked of armour, "that it was an excellent invention, for it not only saved the life of the wearer, but prevented his hurting anybody else."

What has also influenced the commencement of this history at this era is, that there is no authentic information regarding the dress of the Artillery until the date 1642. Uniformity in dress did not, however, come into vogue until much later, the first mention of any uniform of Artillery being in the year 1685, as given hereafter.

The question of strict uniformity in dress does not seem to have excited much attention in the British Army previous to the date 1815; therefore many divergences in the mode of wearing certain articles and details of dress may be noticed in prints and portraits of the same date. Commanding Officers were given great latitude, and individual Officers wore practically what they wished.

It will be noted that blue has ever been the colour of an artilleryman's coat. The reason of this is hard to discover, unless, as it has been suggested, regiments of

INTRODUCTION.

cavalry and infantry alone were originally entitled to wear the royal scarlet, being the servants of the sovereign, whilst artillerymen, being merely the servants of the various officials of the ordnance, did not enjoy this privilege. It is probable that when it was found necessary, for purposes of discipline and service generally, to clothe them uniformly, the sister-colour of blue was adopted, and blue was soon generally recognized as belonging to the Artillery. This point is well illustrated by the following passage from "Zeluco," by Dr. John Moore (the father of Sir John Moore):—

"The Swiss Guards are stout men, clothed in scarlet, the same as our soldiers; but they have moustaches on their lips, like the rat-catchers in St. Giles'. The French Foot Guards are dressed in blue, and all marching regiments in white, which has a very foolish appearance for soldiers, and as for blue regimentals, they are only fit for the Blue Horse and the Artillery" (Dawson's letter, vol. ii. p. 256).

CHARLES I.

1625—1649.

THE luxuriousness of the manners and customs of the Court stamped itself on the minds of the people of England, and a visible sign of the extravagance of this reign was manifest in the costume of the period.

The pictures painted by Vandyke at this time have so immortalized the period, that we who come later are influenced by this master's brush, and generally designate the costume worn at this period as "Vandyke dress."

This was an age of the extremes of elegance and the picturesque, and never before or since have they been carried to such an extent in England.

It was not until about the middle of Charles's reign that the height of fashion was reached; old customs and old clothes die hard, and the influence of James I.'s reign was felt long after Charles I. ascended the throne. The nations of Europe all contributed to make the costume of the period what it was.

IRON HAT OR POT, TIME OF CHARLES I.

Generally speaking, the dress of a Cavalier consisted of a doublet of silk, satin, or velvet, with large loose sleeves slashed up the front, the collar covered by a falling band of lace, and a short cloak over the shoulders. Long breeches, fringed or pointed round the bottoms, met the tops of the wide boots. Broad-leafed Flemish hats of beaver, with richly laced hat-bands and plumes of falling

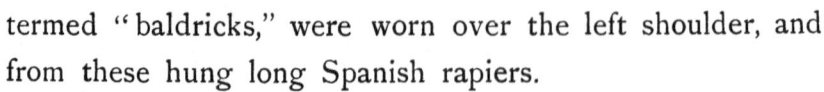

feathers. The hair was worn long and curled, falling on either side of the face. Moustaches and chin tuft were also the fashion. Very richly embroidered sword-belts, termed "baldricks," were worn over the left shoulder, and from these hung long Spanish rapiers.

This costume was well enough for the piping times of peace, and for lounging about the gay salons of the Court; but in time of war it was exchanged for a richly laced buff coat, encircled by a broad scarf tied in an enormous bow. This was a more serviceable costume than the peacock-like one previously described. Armour was beginning to be left off, but generally Officers wore a cuirass over the buff coat.

Charles I. wished greatly to create military efficiency, and strove hard to bring about much-needed reforms in his army. He wrote a Military Code in 1640, and also took great pains in trying to bring about some uniformity in the fashion of armour and arms of his Officers and men, a circumstance never before attended to. The modern firelock was invented in this reign, dating from 1635.

"The personal equipment of a gunner at about this date comprised horn (for priming-powder), priming-iron, compasses, plummet and quadrant (for directing pieces), piece of chalk, tape or measured string, level (for testing mortar platform). The matross carried dagger, snaphance, musquett, and half-pike: the dagger was screwed into the muzzle of the musquett at close quarters." *

* "Memoirs Historical and Biographical," by Major and Quarter-Master R. H. Murdoch, R.A., P.R.A.I., Vol. xx.

AUTHORITIES.—"Ye Gunner's Glasse, 1642." By Master-Gunner Eldred.
Grose's "Military Antiquities."
Meyrick's "Antient Armour."
Luard's "History of the Dress of the British Soldier."

CHARLES I.

This drawing depicts an artilleryman during the reign of Charles I., and is the earliest period about which authentic information can be obtained. The principal authority is a very rare old work in the R.A. Library, Woolwich, entitled "Ye Gunner's Glasse, 1642," by William Eldred, sometime Master Gunner of Dover Castle.

The frontispiece in this work consists of a portrait of the author in the dress of the period. It is a woodcut, and is coloured—coat blue, facings scarlet, lace yellow; but at what date this colouring was done it is impossible to say. Master-Gunner Eldred is shown holding in his hand a linstock and a pair of calipers, or compasses, for gauging the shot.

THE COMMONWEALTH.

1649—1660.

UNDER the rule of Cromwell, fashions in dress underwent a change which was carried to the opposite extreme to that in the reign of Charles I. The grim sobriety of the Puritanical element was visible in the outward garb; at all events, there was an affectation of what was then considered godliness in the dress of Cromwell's party.

They close-cropped their heads, and this gave rise to the nickname, invented by the

A GORGET.

PURITAN HAT.

Cavalier party, of "Roundheads," in contrast to their method of wearing the hair long. Puritan hats of beaver were worn quite plain and guiltless of any ornamentation, buff coats with a cuirass or large gorget covered the body, and occasionally helmets of steel were worn.

Large wide-topped boots, with huge spurs, completed the dress of a soldier at this period.

AUTHORITIES.—Grose's "Military Antiquities."
Meyrick's "Antient Armour."
Luard's "History of the Dress of the British Soldier."

CHARLES II.
1660—1685.

CHARLES II., at the Restoration, disbanded the army and raised a body of Life Guards, consisting of two regiments; this formed the nucleus of our present standing army. The practice of clothing soldiers by regiments in one uniform dress was not introduced by Louis XIV. until 1665, and did not become general in our army for many years afterwards.

The following description gives a very good idea of the fashions of this interesting period:—

"A strange effeminate age when men strive to imitate women in their apparell, viz. long periwigs, patches on their faces, painting, short wide breeches like petticoats, muffs, and their clothes highly scented, bedecked with ribbons of all colours. And this apparell was not only used by gentlemen and others of inferior quality, but by souldiers, especially those of the Life Gard to the King, who would have spanners * hanging on one side and a muff on the other, and when dirty weather, some of them would relieve their gards in pattens.

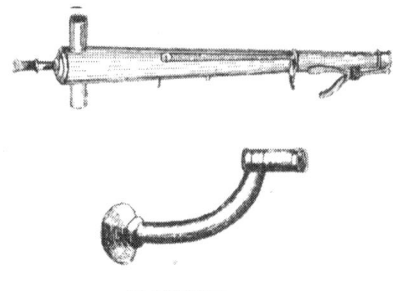

SPANNERS.

"On the other side, women would strive to be like men, viz. when they rode on horseback or in coaches, weare plush caps like monteros, either full of ribbons or feathers, long periwigs which men used to weare, and riding coate of a red colour, all bedaubed with lace, which they call vests; and this habit was chiefly used by the ladies and maids of honour belonging to the Queen, brought in fashion about Anno 1662, which they were at this time, 1665, at their being in Oxon." †

* For spanning or winding up the spring of the wheel-lock.

† Wood's "Life and Times (at Oxford)," vol. i., Dec. 1663. *Vide* Pepys' "Diary," Jan. 10, 166$\frac{5}{6}$; July 27, 1665; Jan. 11, 1666.

The hats were worn very large, with feathers, the crowns low, and the brims turned up. This led, as will be noted in Queen Anne's reign, to the cocked hat of the eighteenth century. For protection from sabre cuts and blows, a small steel cap was sewn inside the crown of the hat. Very large boots with wide tops to them, to prevent the leg being crushed in a charge, were worn, these boots being called "gambadoes." At this time officers often wore no other armour than a large gorget, which almost served the purpose of a breast-plate.

In the historical novel of "Peveril of the Peak," vol. iii. p. 243, we are told—

"that, to protect the Protestants against dreaded assassinations by the Papists at this time, and to avoid the inconvenience of breasts and back-plates of steel, some ingenious artist, probably belonging to the Mercers' Company, had contrived what was called the silk armour, being composed of a doublet and breeches of quilted silk, so closely stitched and of such thickness as to be proof against bullet or steel; while a thick bonnet of the same materials, with ear-flaps attached to it, protected the head. The whole was of a dusky orange colour."

The Honourable Roger North, speaking of the Green Ribbon Club, says—

"There was much recommendation of the silk armour, and the prudence of being provided with it, against the time that Protestants were to be massacred. And, accordingly, there were abundance of those silken back, breast, and potts made and sold, that were pretended to be pistol proof; in which any man dressed up, was as safe as in a house, for it was impossible any one could go to strike him for laughing, so ridiculous was the figure, as they say, of hogs in armour; an image of derision insensible, but to the view as I have had it."*

The drawing of silk armour is copied from a plate in Grose's "Ancient Armour," and is described by him as follows:—

"A curious suit of armour belonging to Mr. Cosway, of the age of King James or

---

* Meyrick's "Antient Armour."

CHARLES II.

Charles I. It is said to be tilting armour, but from the circumstance of having the back-piece made strongly defensible, seems rather to have been intended for military service, as in tilting no strokes might have been levelled at the back. The whole is covered with a cinnamon-coloured silk, and is strongly quilted and stuffed; besides

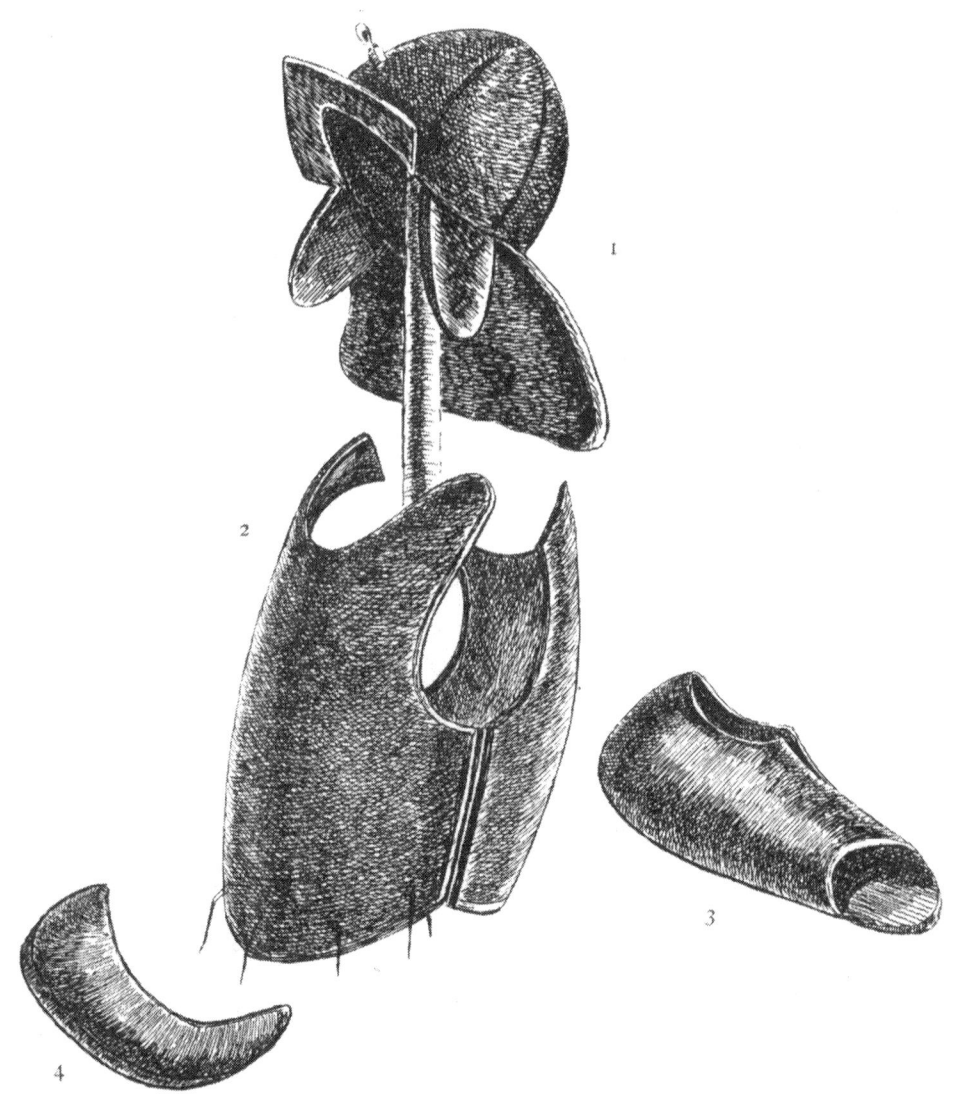

SILK ARMOUR.
(1) HEAD-PIECE; (2) BREAST AND BACK; (3) COVERING FOR LEFT ARM; (4) TASSET ON SKIRT.

which, it seems strengthened either with jacked leather or thin iron plates, sewed on in the nature of a brigandine.

"The head-piece has also an iron cap between the outside and lining. Most probably this suit is what was called *silk armour*—a species often mentioned in history, and found in the inventory of ancient armories."

    Consisted of—The head-piece.
                    The breast and back.
                    The tasset, or skirt.
                    The covering for the left arm, curiously stuffed and quilted, intended to answer the use of a shield.

AUTHORITIES.—Grose's "Military Antiquities."
                Meyrick's "Antient Armour."
                Luard's "History of the Dress of the British Soldier."
                "Armies of To-day, 1893." ("The Standing Army of Great Britain," by General Viscount Wolseley.)

JAMES II.

1685—1688.

THE costume remained much the same in this reign as in that of Charles II., but was not quite so ornate.

Perukes were the feature of this period, and are said to have originated from the fact that Charles II., when a boy, wore his hair in long waving curls upon his shoulders; his courtiers, to imitate and flatter their young sovereign, wore wigs of false hair in imitation of his natural curls. The king, when he grew up, paid his courtiers the compliment of imitating them, and wore a peruke, and thus this absurd fashion gained a firm footing—so firm, indeed, that during the reign of William III. and Anne it was carried to such an extent that perukes grew to an enormous size, and were considered the chief feature in the toilet.

Military men, of course, were forced to follow the fashion set them by their sovereign. And no one that looks at portraits of this period can fail to be struck with the incongruity of such an eminently unsuitable mode of wearing the hair for soldiers undergoing the hardships of a campaign.

The helmets of steel for purposes of war were seldom worn, and large beaver hats, with turned-up brims and ornamented with feathers, took their place.

During this reign, for the first time, is found a written description of the dress and equipment of gunners and matrosses of the train of Artillery, as follows:—

"On June 21, 1685, a second warrant was issued to the Master-General, directing him to have in readiness a train of artillery, '*necessary at this juncture of*

PLATE I.

AN OFFICER AND ARTILLERYMAN OR MATROSS, TRAIN OF ARTILLERY.
1660—1702.

Description of Plate.

THE figure on the left depicts an Officer of the Train of Artillery during this period. He wears the large felt hat and feathers which succeeded the helmet of steel, but generally a small steel cap was sewn inside the hat for protection from sabre-cuts.

The hair was worn curled, falling on the shoulders, and generally ending in two love-locks; but during the reigns of James II. and his successors down to George II., perukes were worn, which were made of false hair to imitate long waving curls.

The steel cuirass was still worn, and was discontinued about the time George I. came to the throne. At this time it was the custom to wear it outside the coat.

The boots of the period were of that large heavy kind called "gambadoes," having very large tops to them, to prevent the leg being crushed in a charge.

On the right is shown an artilleryman or matross, carrying his linstock, with which to fire the gun.

He wears a broad belt or girdle round his waist of neat's leather, from which depends his brass-hilted hanger or cutlass, and across his shoulders is slung a powder-horn and a pouch or wallet.

Our soldiers, up to the time of Frederick the Great, always stood on parade, when at the position of attention, with their legs apart.

AUTHORITIES.—"History of the British Standing Army, A.D. 1660–1700." By Colonel Clifford Walton, C.B.

Cleaveland's "Notes on the Early History of the Royal Artillery."

Grose's "Military Antiquities."

Meyrick's "Antient Armour."

Luard's "History of the Dress of the British Soldier."

Details, Colours.—Warrant 1689, signed by Schomberg for gunners, etc.

Style of Dress, etc.—Van Wyck's "Boyne;" Mallet, "St. Remy," etc.

Arms and Accoutrements.—In Brit. Mus. Add. MSS. 5795. In Harl. MSS. 7458-63, States of Ordnance Stores, 1687-91, appear, "powder-horns and linstocks for matrosses, and girdles of neat's leather with brass buckles for bombardiers."

NOTE.—The matrosses' and gunners' swords formed a portion of the clothing.

Orders for dress as quoted in text.

JAMES II.

time, when divers traitors and rebels are in open hostilities against us,' consisting of sixteen pieces of brass ordnance, with the requisite stores, ammunition, and equipage from the stores in his charge, with all expedition, to march towards Chippenham, in Wiltshire, to join the Earl of Feversham, whose orders the Officers of the said train were to obey and observe.

"The following brass pieces composed this train, viz. :—

> 2 Twelve-prs.
> 4 Demi-culverins.
> 4 Six-prs.
> 4 Sakers.
> 2 Minions.
> Total, 16.

"The men attached to the train were armed as follows, viz. :—

> 2 gunners' mates } each a field-stave.*
> 32 gunners
>
> 32 matrosses: each a half-pike, and a hanger with belt.
>
> Sergeant of pioneers: a partizan, and a hanger with belt.
>
> Pioneer corporal: a halbert, and hanger with belt.
>
> 20 pioneers: each a hanger and belt, and between them { 8 pickaxes. 6 shovels. 6 spades. }
>
> Drummer: a drum, and hanger with belt.
>
> Hangers with belts for the conductors, wheelers, carpenters, coopers, smiths, and collar-makers.

"The pioneers attached to the train were clothed in red jackets and red caps, and the artificers in red clothes, laced."

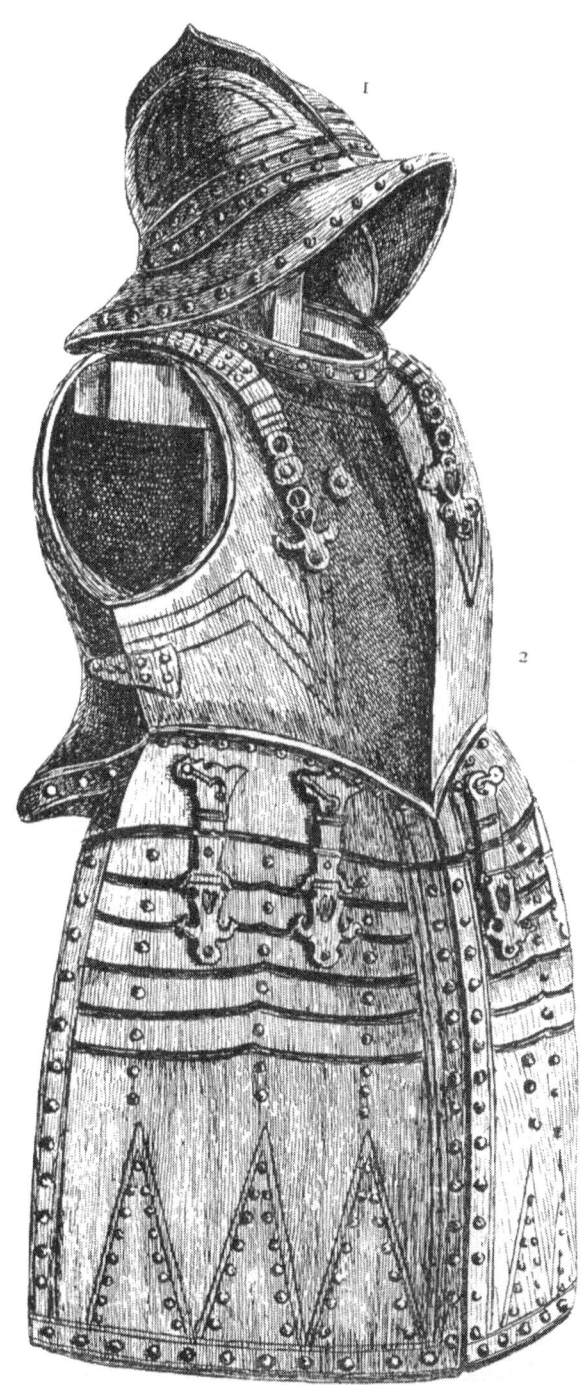

(1) IRON HAT OR POT; (2) A SUIT OF BLACK HARQUEBUSS ARMOUR.

* *Field-stave*, "linstock."

Oct. 27.—"From the Tower, armour lent to Colonel William Legg, for his own use, by order of the Board of Ordnance :—

Harquebuss armour, carbine-proof { Backs 2   Pott 1
                                   Breasts ... 2   Gauntlet ... 1 "

Oct. 30.—"To Jacob Richards, for his own use in the Train of Artillery, by order of the Board :—

    Silk armour ... ... 1 suit."

"On November 1, 1688, the Prince of Orange landed in England, and a train of 26 pieces was immediately organized to 'attend his Majesty's forces, consisting of 15,000 foot and 5000 horse.' The warrant for this train bears date November 8, 1688, although a preparatory warrant was issued in the previous month."

The matrosses on this service were clothed as under :—
    Striped jackets and breeches.
    Blue stockings.
    Leather caps.

The pioneers :—

Red cloth coats.	Woollen stockings.
Red kersey breeches.	Shoes and buckles.
Leather Montreur caps.	Neckcloths.

Conductors : red cloth cloaks.
The chief engineer : a suit of silk armour.
The matrosses were armed with half-pikes and hangers.

1688. *Dec.* 1.—"To Sir Martin Beckman, lent him for his own use, by order of the Board :—

    Silk armour ... ... 1 suit."

(Cleaveland's Notes.)

AUTHORITIES.—Luard's "History of the Dress of the British Soldier."
    Cleaveland's "Notes on the Early History of the Royal Regiment of Artillery."
    Grose's "Military Antiquities."
    Colonel Clifford Walton, C.B., "History of the British Standing Army, A.D. 1660-1700."

JAMES II.

time, when divers traitors and rebels are in open hostilities against us,' consisting of sixteen pieces of brass ordnance, with the requisite stores, ammunition, and equipage from the stores in his charge, with all expedition, to march towards Chippenham, in Wiltshire, to join the Earl of Feversham, whose orders the Officers of the said train were to obey and observe.

"The following brass pieces composed this train, viz. :—

- 2 Twelve-prs.
- 4 Demi-culverins.
- 4 Six-prs.
- 4 Sakers.
- 2 Minions.
- Total, 16.

"The men attached to the train were armed as follows, viz. :—

- 2 gunners' mates } each a field-stave.*
- 32 gunners
- 32 matrosses: each a half-pike, and a hanger with belt.
- Sergeant of pioneers: a partizan, and a hanger with belt.
- Pioneer corporal: a halbert, and hanger with belt.
- 20 pioneers: each a hanger and belt, and between them { 8 pickaxes. 6 shovels. 6 spades.
- Drummer: a drum, and hanger with belt.
- Hangers with belts for the conductors, wheelers, carpenters, coopers, smiths, and collar-makers.

"The pioneers attached to the train were clothed in red jackets and red caps, and the artificers in red clothes, laced."

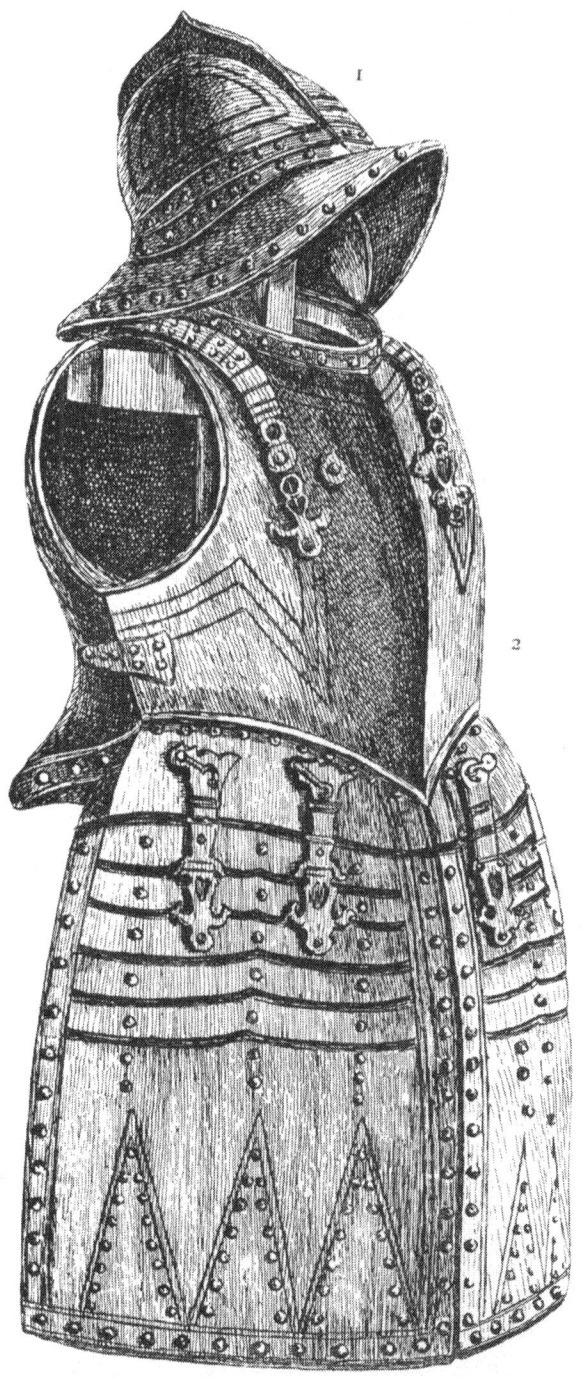

(1) IRON HAT OR POT; (2) A SUIT OF BLACK HARQUEBUSS ARMOUR.

* *Field-stave,* "linstock."

Oct. 27.—"From the Tower, armour lent to Colonel William Legg, for his own use, by order of the Board of Ordnance :—

Harquebuss armour, carbine-proof { Backs ... 2   Pott ... 1
                                    Breasts ... 2   Gauntlet ... 1 "

Oct. 30.—"To Jacob Richards, for his own use in the Train of Artillery, by order of the Board :—

Silk armour ... ... 1 suit."

"On November 1, 1688, the Prince of Orange landed in England, and a train of 26 pieces was immediately organized to 'attend his Majesty's forces, consisting of 15,000 foot and 5000 horse.' The warrant for this train bears date November 8, 1688, although a preparatory warrant was issued in the previous month."

The matrosses on this service were clothed as under :—

Striped jackets and breeches.
Blue stockings.
Leather caps.

The pioneers :—

Red cloth coats.   Woollen stockings.
Red kersey breeches.   Shoes and buckles.
Leather Montreur caps.   Neckcloths.

Conductors : red cloth cloaks.
The chief engineer : a suit of silk armour.
The matrosses were armed with half-pikes and hangers.

1688. *Dec.* 1.—"To Sir Martin Beckman, lent him for his own use, by order of the Board :—

Silk armour ... ... 1 suit."

(Cleaveland's Notes.)

AUTHORITIES.—Luard's "History of the Dress of the British Soldier."
Cleaveland's "Notes on the Early History of the Royal Regiment of Artillery."
Grose's "Military Antiquities."
Colonel Clifford Walton, C.B., "History of the British Standing Army, A.D. 1660-1700."

WILLIAM AND MARY.

1688—1702.

FASHION in dress remained very much the same in this reign as in the one preceding it. Perukes remained in full fashion, and they grew to be of an enormous size—so much so, indeed, that the face was almost hidden under them. Cuirasses, gorgets, and breastplates protected the body and gambadoes the legs of the soldiers at this period. Harquebuss armour, as will be seen from the ensuing extracts, still continued to be worn. The fashions were very cumbrous and ungainly, and more suited to mounted men than to foot-soldiers.

"King James II., having fled the kingdom on December 23, 1688, landed at Kinsale, in Ireland, with a French force of about 5000 men, in March, 1689. Consequently, on June 1, a warrant was issued for a train to be prepared for shipment to Ireland. For this train, besides various other ordnance stores, an additional proportion of ordnance and other stores demanded by his Grace the Duke of Schomberg:—

Brass ordnance mounted on travelling carriages, complete } Culverins 6

"With spare carriages, stores, ammunition, harness, and cloths for pioneers, as follows:—

Large blue coats, lined with orange-colour 40
Orange-coloured waistcoats 40

HISTORY OF THE DRESS OF THE ROYAL ARTILLERY.

Blue breeches	40 pairs
Stockings	40 pairs
Caps, embroidered with shovel in front	40
For two sergeants	2
For two drummers	2
For a corporal	1
Drivers	200
Cloaths for the drivers' suits	200
Oats, beans, and hay for the train horses, being in No.	500
Master-smith and his assistants	14 "

(Cleaveland's Notes.)

Arms, etc., for the gunners and matrosses:—

Halberts	3
Short pikes	80
Hangers with belts	30
Long carbines, straped	146
Cartouch boxes for do.	146
Pistols	50 pairs
Troop saddles	18
Bitt bridles	18

(Brit. Mus. Add. MSS. 5795.)

1689. *July* 16.—" The Duke of Schomberg appointed Mr. George Barnard waggon-master to this office, and to attend the train of artillery designed for Ireland.

" The Duke ordered that the gunners, mattrosses, and tradesmen have coats of blue, with brass buttons, and lined with orange bayes,* and hatts with orange silk galoone.

" The carters' grey coats, lined with the same."

1691. *Feb.* 27.—" To Sir Henry Shaw, Lieutenant-General of the late Train of Artillery:—

Harquebuss armour, carbine-proof { Backs ... 1 Pott ... 1
                                    Breast ... 1 Elbow gauntlet 1 "

* *Query* baize.

WILLIAM AND MARY.

1692. *May* 28.—"To Abrah Butler, chief petardier of the Flanders train, per warrant from his Majesty:—

Harquebuss armour, musquet-proof { Back 1
Breast 1
Pott ... ... 1 "

1702. *April* 10.—"Armour delivered for the service of the train now going to sea:—

Harquebuss armour, carbine-proof: Backs 10, breasts 10, potts 10."

(Cleaveland's Notes.)

BACK.

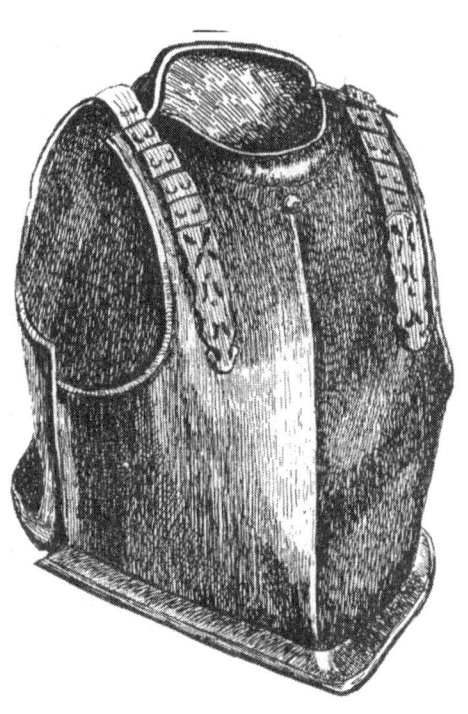

BREAST.

AUTHORITIES.—*Vide* reign of James II.

Plate II.

AN OFFICER, TRAIN OF ARTILLERY.

1702—1714.

Description of Plate.

This plate represents an Officer of high rank in the Train of Artillery during Marlborough's wars on the continent. He wears a cuirass under his long coat, encircled by a crimson sash; the large cavalry boots called gambadoes, with silver spurs.

A three-cornered laced cocked hat was worn; also a large peruke.

Authorities.—Grose's "Military Antiquities."
Luard's "History of the Dress of the British Soldier."
Portrait of General Borgard, R.A. Circa 1710.
Portrait of Colonel Jonas Watson, R.A. Circa 1710.
Portrait of Captain John Romer, Engineers. 1710.
Orders for dress as quoted in text previously.

ANNE.

1702—1714.

PREVIOUS to this reign, as will have been seen—that is, during the reign of Charles I., the Commonwealth, Charles II., James II., and William III.—very wide-brimmed Flemish hats with curling feathers had been worn by Officers of the Army. As time went on the great inconvenience of these brims began to be perceived, and first one and then two flaps were turned up. About

PERUKE.

the time of Queen Anne the third flap was turned up, and the regular cocked hat of the eighteenth century came into existence.

During this reign chivalric costume can be said to have died out, though cuirasses, gorgets, and breastplates continued to be worn by Officers of Cavalry and Artillery. People of fashion wore cocked hats, though some Officers, still tenacious of old customs, adhered to the wide-brimmed hat turned up on two sides and trimmed with feathers, as was worn in previous reigns.

The hair was worn, by some, tied behind, but generally very large perukes were the fashion.

"Square-cut coats and long-flapped waistcoats, with large pockets to both; the stockings drawn up over the knee so high as to hide the breeches, but gartered below it; large hanging cuffs and laced ruffles; the skirts of the coats stiffened out with wire or buckram, from behind which peeped the hilt of the sword, deprived of the broad and splendid belt from which it swung in the preceding reigns; blue or scarlet stockings, with gold or silver clocks; lace neckcloths; square-toed, short-quartered shoes, with high heels and small buckles; very long and formally curled perukes, black riding-wigs, long wigs, and night-cap wigs; small three-cornered hats laced with gold or silver galloon, and sometimes trimmed with feathers, composed the habit of the noblemen and gentlemen." (Luard's " History.")

Queen Anne was very strict in matters of detail of the dress of her courtiers. It is told of her that "she once sent for Lord Bolingbroke in haste, who immediately attended in a Ramilies tie instead of a full-bottomed wig, at which she was greatly offended."

This is the noted Lord Bolingbroke to whom is attributed the introduction of the fashion of "tying" the hair.

AUTHORITIES.—*Vide* reign of James II.

GEORGE I

1714—1727.

HE Royal Regiment of Artillery was formed on May 26, 1716. The uniform consisted of blue, faced with scarlet. The Officers wore scarlet waistcoats and breeches.

The character of the uniforms in the early part of this reign remained very much the same as in that of Queen Anne, but perukes had fallen entirely out of fashion. They were succeeded by the tie wig and the bob wig, and these again by the Ramilies tail and the pig-tail. Clubs were also worn. This was done by having the head well pomatumed or larded and powdered; the thick tail was turned up, leaving a large knob below, and it was secured by a leathern strap. This was termed wearing the hair "clubbed."

RAMILIES HAT AND TIE.

HAIR CLUBBED.

AUTHORITIES. — Grose's "Military Antiquities."
Luard's "History of the Dress of the British Soldier."

R.A. OFFICER, TIME OF GEORGE I., 1714-1727.

GEORGE II.

1727—1760.

THIS was a period of heaviness and slowness in military movement, and the uniform and accoutrements were cumbersome in the extreme. Particular attention, as will be seen from the various orders of dress, was paid to the dressing of the hair and the "cock" of the hat. Pig-tails were adopted about the year 1745.

There are two portraits extant of Officers of the Train of Artillery when first regimented, namely, of Major-General Albert Borgard and of Lieut.-Colonel Jonas Watson, both about the date 1730. These Officers are represented in half-armour, wearing the breastplate, which was not entirely discontinued even to the time of George III., who in his first coinage also wears a breastplate.

Portrait-painters, at the beginning of the eighteenth century, always dressed their subjects, if they were military men, in armour. General Borgard was the last Artillery Officer who wore body-armour, which is depicted in the above-mentioned portrait. During this reign sashes were worn over the shoulders.

Officers at this period always carried, besides swords, fusees, much in the same way that a Highland chief, at the beginning of the present century, carried a gun. These fusees were, no doubt, highly prized at the time, on account of their rarity and monetary value.

The principal head-dresses worn by military men were the Ramilies cocked-hat, and the larger one styled the Kevenhuller.

ORDERS OF DRESS.

1743.—" The uniform dress of the Officers was a plain blue coat, lined with scarlet, a large scarlet Argyle cuff, double breasted, and with yellow buttons to the bottom of the skirts; scarlet waistcoat and breeches, the waistcoat trimmed with broad gold lace, and a gold-laced hat. The sergeants' coats were trimmed, the lappels, cuffs, and pockets, with a broad single gold lace; the corporals' and bombardiers' with a narrow single gold lace. The gunners and matrosses, plain blue coats; all the non-commissioned officers and privates having scarlet half-lappels, scarlet cuffs, and slashed sleeves with five buttons, and blue waistcoats and breeches; the sergeants' hats trimmed with a broad, and the other non-commissioned officers and privates with a narrow, gold lace. White spatterdashes were then worn. The regimental clothing was delivered to the non-commissioned officers and privates only once a year, excepting regimental coats, which they received every second year, and the intermediate year a coarse blue surtout, which served for laboratory work, cooking, fatigues, etc., and was delivered with the usual small mounting. The arms of the Officers were fusees without bayonets, and not uniform. The sergeants, corporals, and bombardiers were armed with halberts and long brass-hilted swords." (Cleaveland's Notes.) "The gunners carried field-staffs about 2 feet longer than a halbert, with two linstock cocks branching out at the head, and a spear projecting between and beyond them. Great attention was paid to keeping these very bright. A buff belt over the left shoulder, slinging a large powder-horn mounted with brass over the right pocket, and the same long brass-hilted swords as worn by the non-commissioned officers. The matrosses had only common muskets and bayonets and cartouche boxes." (Macbean's MSS.)

The Officers did not then practise saluting with the fusee, and only pulled off their hats as the Duke passed them. (Cleaveland's Notes.)

1747. *March* 2.—

"That none of the men be suffered to go to work in their regimental coats, but either in frocks or surtouts."

1749.—

"The guard to mount to-morrow in black spatterdashes, and the Officers in boots."

Before the army took the field this year, the gunners' field-staves, powder-horns with slings, and swords, and the matrosses' muskets, were laid aside, and both these ranks were armed with carbines and bayonets; all the non-commissioned officers still continued to have halberts. (Cleaveland's Notes.)

PLATE III.

AN OFFICER AND GUNNER, ROYAL ARTILLERY.

1743.

Description of Plate.

This represents a typically Georgian style of dress.

The figure on the left is an Officer, and on the right is a gunner, of the period.

The Officer carried as arms a fusee and gold-hilted sword. His crimson silk sash was very long and broad, having a hole at each end. A pole could be run through the two ends, and a hammock formed in which to carry the Officer off the field if wounded.

The description in detail of the dress of both Officer and gunner is given on pp. 22, 23.*

* See Order of Dress, Kane's List.

Authorities.—Two Water-colour Sketches in "The Cloathing of H.M. Forces." 1743.
   Orders for Dress as quoted in text.

GEORGE II.

1749. *March* 27.—Garrison Order by Colonel Belford:—

"That the captains provide their men with one pair of white stockings each, in which they are to parade at all times when not under arms."

April 3.—

"The non-commissioned officers and men are to be forthwith provided with one good pair of white spatterdashes, with black buttons, also with one pair of black spatterdashes, and a rose to their hair, 'the same as we had in Flanders.'"

This was the first time black spatterdashes were worn in the army. (Cleaveland's Notes.)

1750.—The regimentals of the non-commissioned officers and men underwent an alteration. The sergeants' coats were laced round the button-holes with gold looping, other non-commissioned officers' and men's with yellow worsted. The corporals and bombardiers had gold and worsted shoulder-knots. The *surtouts* were laid aside, and complete suits of clothing were delivered every year. From this time to 1802 the sergeants were distinguished by two gold lace shoulder-knots, a corporal by two of worsted, and a bombardier by one, afterwards by chevrons, as at present. (Kane's List.)

Garrison Order by Colonel Belford:—

"Officers are, for the future, to mount guard in their regimentals, with their fusees and cartouch boxes."

1750. *March* 30:—

"The sergeant of the main guard is not to suffer any non-commissioned officer or private man to go out of the Warren Gate, unless they are dressed clean, their hair combed and tied up, with clean stockings, and shoes well blacked."

July 17:—

"The Commanding Officers of companies are ordered by the General to provide proper wigs for such of their respective men that do not wear their hair, as soon as possible."

1751. *April* 5.—Garrison Order by Colonel Belford:—

"The Officers, when on duty, are to wear the knots of their sashes in their left pocket, with the fringe hanging out."

1753. *February* 6:—

"The Officers are to appear in regimental hats under arms, and no others."

PLATE IV.

AN OFFICER OF THE ROYAL ARTILLERY.

1760.

Description of Plate.

This was the style of dress worn at Minden, and differed but slightly from the uniform of 1743.

Officers still carried fusees.

The gorget signified that the Officer was on duty, and was worn over the waistcoat.

Authorities.—Engraving, "Portrait of Captain Tiffin, R.A., at Minden."
Portrait of Colonel Griffiths Williams, R.A. Circa 1760.
Portrait of Thos. Hosmer, R.A. Circa 1760.
Orders for dress as quoted in text.

GEORGE II.

February 19 :—

"The Officers appointed to inspect the several squads are to review them once every week for the future; to see that every man has 4 good shirts, 4 stocks, 4 pairs of stockings, 2 pairs of white and 1 pair of black spatterdashes, 2 pairs of shoes, etc., and that their arms, accoutrements and clothes are in the best order."

1754. *January* 2 :—

"No Officer to appear under arms in a bob wig for the future."

1754.—Halberts were taken from the corporals and bombardiers, and they fell into the ranks with carbines. (Cleaveland's Notes.)

July 16.—Garrison Order :—

"No non-commissioned officer or private soldier is to appear in ruffles at the review."

1755. *August* 8 :—

"It is ordered that no non-commissioned officer or soldier shall for the future go out of the Warren Gate without their hats being cocked, their hair well combed, tied, and dressed in a regimental manner, their shoes blacked, and clean in every respect."

1756. *February* 13 :—

"Captains are forthwith to provide their respective companies with a knapsack and haversack, each man."

March 31 :—

"The Officers are desired not to appear on parade for the future with hats otherwise cocked than in the 'Cumberland manner.'"

1756. *May* 1 :—

"It is Colonel Belford's orders that no non-commissioned officer or private man is to wear ruffles on their wrists when under arms, or any duty whatever for the future."

1756. *September* 15.—Regimental Order, Byfleet Camp, by Colonel Belford :—

"The non-commissioned officers and men are on all occasions, for the future, to wear their hair clubbed."

1758.—Various orders of dress are given. Boots for the Officers, and black spatterdashes for the men, were the ordinary covering for the extremities on parade, white spatterdashes with their 36 buttons being reserved for grand occasions. (Duncan's History.)

1758. *May* 4.—General Orders:—

"It is the Master-General's order that the uniform waistcoats for the Officers' regimental frocks are to be of plain scarlet cloth, without lace."

Officers discontinued carrying fusees the following year. (Kane's List.)

GEORGE III.

1760—1820.

IT is difficult to distinguish what was the most striking feature in regard to costume during this long reign. A comparison of the style in vogue in 1760 with that of 1820 gives a very fair idea of the enormous changes that occurred during this reign. Military costume had begun, about the year 1800, to emerge from the mediæval style that had characterized it up to that date.

In the early part of this reign hats and wigs were perhaps the most striking and varied features. Hats were worn with very broad brims turned up, or, as it was termed, "cocked." Wigs had been diminishing in size since the reigns previous to George III., and in this reign the practice of frizzing, curling, plastering, and powdering the hair came into fashion.

The common soldiers were perfect slaves to this practice, and were compelled to appear on parade with curled and plastered hair, and long tails hanging down behind. The Officers used pomatum, but the privates used the end of a tallow candle to keep their hair in order.

All sorts and descriptions of methods of dressing the hair succeeded each other; at one time very short tails would be worn, at another the tails would be clubbed, and macaroni tails and pig-tails had their turn also. General Mercer's MS. Notes (see p. 49) give a detailed description of the way the toilet was performed at the end of the eighteenth and beginning of the nineteenth centuries.

The tails grew to an enormous length, and in the year 1804 an order was issued to the Army to reduce them to seven inches. In 1808 the queues of the Army were ordered to be dispensed with. This order was obeyed with the promptest alacrity, but the day after the order was given a counter-order came; by this time, however, the queues were gone. This only tends to show how tenacious of old

PLATE V.

AN OFFICER OF THE ROYAL ARTILLERY.

1764.

DESCRIPTION OF PLATE.

SINCE the date of the last plate, the colour of the waistcoat and breeches was changed from scarlet to buff; otherwise the style of the dress remained unaltered.

AUTHORITIES.—Portrait of Captain John Godwin, R.A. Circa 1764.
Miniature of an Cfficer R.A. (no name or date). Circa 1764.
Orders for dress as quoted in text.

and useless customs the authorities were. How such an unmilitary and unwarlike method of dressing the hair had lasted for so many years, it is quite impossible to understand.

On August 1, 1808, his Majesty's orders for the Army to dispense with the use of queues were directed by the Master-General to be extended to the Artillery (*vide* Orders of this date). Regarding queues and powder, we learn that—

"To such an excess was this carried during the command of the late Duke of Kent at Gibraltar, that when a field-day was ordered, there not being sufficient barbers in the garrison to attend all the Officers in the morning, the seniors claimed the privilege of their rank; the juniors consequently were obliged to have their heads dressed the night before, and to preserve the beauty of this artistic arrangement, pomatumed, powdered, curled, and clubbed, these poor fellows were obliged to sleep on their faces!

"It is said that in the adjutant's office of each regiment there was kept a pattern of the correct curls, to which the barbers could refer." *

The many changes that occurred in Artillery uniform during this long reign will be given in their order, together with the authorities for the details of the plates.

Orders of Dress.

1763. *June* 25.—Garrison Order by Colonel Williamson:—

"They are the General's Orders that the non-commissioned officers and men of all the companies wear their hair plaited, and when short clubbed, and in no other way whatsoever."

1764. *January* 24.—Garrison Orders:—

"Those Officers who are not provided with full regimentals are to make them up immediately with buff waistcoats and breeches."

1768. White waistcoats and breeches were adopted, instead of buff. (Kane's List.)

1770. *February* 1.—Garrison Orders by Lieut.-Colonel Godwin:—

"When the regiment is ordered to appear with arms, it is expected that the Officers shall always appear with fusees."

February 25.—By Major-General Williamson:—

"The Officers' regimentals are to be laced with the same sort of lace as the last regimentals, with epaulettes instead of laced shoulder-knots."

* Luard's "History of the British Soldier."

PLATE VI.

AN OFFICER OF THE ROYAL ARTILLERY.

1778.

DESCRIPTION OF PLATE.

WHITE waistcoats and breeches were now worn; sashes, round the waist, instead of diagonally over the shoulder. The uniform was less cumbrous than heretofore.

AUTHORITIES.—Portrait of Captain Patterson, R.A. Circa 1778.
Portrait of Colonel Stehelin, R.A. Circa 1778.
Pencil sketch of an Officer R.A. 1778.
Miniature of an Officer R.A. (no name or date). Circa 1778.
Orders for dress as quoted in text.

GEORGE III.

April 20. General Orders :—

"His Majesty has consented that the Officers of the Regiment shall no longer have fusees when under arms, but drawn swords, with which they are to salute, the same as the Dragoon Officers."

April 26.—Garrison Orders by Major-General Williamson :—

"The non-commissioned officers, gunners, and private men's hair is to be plaited and turned up behind with a black ribbon or tape, three-quarters of a yard long, in a bow knot at the tye. Those men who have their hair so short that it will not plait, must be provided, as soon as possible, with a false plait."

This year the German mode of wearing the sash round the waist was introduced, instead of over the right shoulder. (Kane's List.)

1771. *December* 7.—Garrison Orders by Major-General Williamson :—

"It is General Williamson's orders that the Officers of the 2nd Battalion do provide themselves with plain frocks and plain hats, with a gold band, button, and loop."

1772. *March* 11.—Garrison Order prohibits any alteration in the clothing of the men, or uniform of the Officers, or discipline of any Battalion, without the previous knowledge and approbation of the Master-General. (Kane's List.)

May 15.—Garrison Order by Colonel Cleaveland :—

"It is expected that the Captains, or Commanding Officers of companies, will have their men completed with white linen breeches by the latter end of next week."

May 28.—Battalion Orders by Colonel Cleaveland :—

"The 4th Battalion to be under arms to-morrow. The men to be in white breeches, white stockings, black half-spatterdashes, and their hair clubbed; the Officers in plain frocks, half-spatterdashes, and queues, and to wear white cotton or thread stockings under their half-spatterdashes. The Officers to have a gold button and loop to their plain hats."

June 28.—General Orders :—

"General Conway has been pleased to order, that for the future the accoutrements of the four Battalions of the Royal Regiment of Artillery are to be white instead of buff colour, in conformity to the King's Order."

July 10.—Battalion Orders by Major-General Desaguliers :—

"When the Officers are on duty, they are to have their hair clubbed."

July 11.—Battalion Orders by Major-General Desaguliers :—

"The Officers' hats are to be cocked, and worn in the same manner as the Battalion. The men are to wear their hats with the front loops just over their nose."

Plate VII.

AN OFFICER OF THE ROYAL HORSE ARTILLERY.

1793.

Description of Plate.

Horse Artillery was introduced into the British Army in 1793, the two first troops, A and B, being formed in that year.

The plate shows an Officer of the "Chestnut Troop," in the uniform worn at that date (*vide* Plate XXIII. for centenary).

The hair is worn in a small queue, tied with a few turns of ribbon, and ornamented with a large silk rosette. Both Officers and men used powder.

The head-dress worn was a helmet, similar to the old English Light Dragoon helmet. The turban or fillet surrounding the lower part was of crimson silk; white plumes were worn on the left side of it.

The first Horse Artillery jacket was after the style of the Chasseur jacket of the French Army. It hooked at the collar, and sloped away towards a short skirt (somewhat resembling that of a Light Infantryman's) which terminated it behind, had half facings; and on the shoulders, wings, made of interwoven rings.

Well pipeclayed doe or buck skins, fastened at the knee with buttons, and jack-boots with stiff tops, were worn.

A crimson sash encircled the waist, with a large "boss" or rose (from which the fringes depended) on the left side, in front, and the sash was tied behind under the coat with ribbons.

There was a framework or stiffening in the shabracque to keep the tassels from drooping.

See General Mercer's MS. Notes, pp. 49, 58, 62, 72.

Authorities.—Coloured print, title, "Sadler's Flying Artillery." 1798.
    Miniature of Officer R.H.A. Circa 1793.
    Water-colour sketch in Captain Lawson's "Evolutions of R.H.A." 1793.
    General Mercer's MS. Notes and description of uniform at this period.
    Prints of Light Dragoons in the "British Military Library." 1799.
    Prints of Light Infantry in the "British Military Library." 1799.

GEORGE III.

July 25.—Battalion Orders by Major-General Desaguliers:—

"Black stocks being no more an uniform part of the dress of the Battalion, the Captains, or Commanding Officers of companies, are forthwith to provide their men with white ones."

November 24.—Battalion Orders by Lieut.-Colonel Pattison:—

"The Officers are constantly to mount guard in their plain frocks, plain hats, their regimental swords, and their hair well powdered; and when the men wear whole or half gaiters, the Officers to do the same."

1777. The dress of a gunner about this period was a gold-laced cocked hat, the 4th Battalion wearing a black feather, hair clubbed and powdered, white stock, white breeches, white stockings, and a carbine and bayonet. (Duncan's "History R.A.")

1779. *June* 13.—General Orders:—

"The Officers of the 1st and 3rd Battalions having requested leave to wear shoulder-belts, the Master-General has consented to the same, and they are constantly to be worn upon all duties, agreeably to the custom of the Army."

1782. *October* 25.—The Master-General, His Grace the Duke of Richmond, notified that the uniform of the Regiment was now changed: That the Officers' laced regimentals were to be laid aside, and a plain blue coat, with red facings and cuffs and white lining, substituted. The lining of the men's clothing was also changed from red to white. (Kane's List.)

1782. Equipment of an Artillery subaltern, laid down by the Board of Ordnance:—

1 suit of full uniform.	12 pairs of stockings.
1 frock suit of uniform.	6 linen waistcoats.
1 laced hat.	6 linen breeches.
2 pairs of boots.	12 handkerchiefs.
1 regimental great-coat.	1 pair of pistols.
1 plain hat.	1 regimental sword, belt and clasp.
12 shirts.	1 sash.
12 stocks.	3 pairs of shoes.

(Duncan's "History R.A.")

1782. The contents of gunner's knapsack—

1 canvas painted knapsack.	6 false collars.
4 white shirts.	1 canvas frock.
1 check shirt.	1 canvas pair of trousers.

PLATE VIII.

AN OFFICER AND GUNNER, ROYAL ARTILLERY.

1794.

DESCRIPTION OF PLATE.

ON the left the Officer is shown wearing the curious head-dress of this period; his one epaulette denotes that he is a Company Officer, Field Officers wearing two.

The gunner is wearing his full-dress head-dress, from which was afterwards evolved the cap of the early part of the eighteenth century, and the chako of a later period.

AUTHORITIES.—For description see General Mercer's MS. Notes describing the uniform of the period.

Head-dress.—Portrait of Lieut.-General Congreve. Circa 1795.

Miniature of an Officer R.A. Circa 1795.

GEORGE III.

1 leather cap.
2 pairs of shoes.
1 pair of black cloth gaiters.
1 pair of white stockings (thread).
1 pair of worsted stockings.
3 pairs of Welsh yarn socks.
1 pair of shoe-buckles.
1 powder bag and puff.
1 razor.
1 shaving-box.

1785. *February* 1.—General Orders:—

"The Marching Battalions to conform to the gaiters established for the Army by his Majesty (black cloth), the buttons to be of the same pattern as the regimental waistcoat."

June 25.—General Orders:—

"The Officers' coats are to be made with a round regimental cape, without a standing-up collar. They are to wear plain hats, with a gold chain, loop, and ordnance button of the waistcoat size."

June 29.—General Orders:—

"The Master-General directs that the Officers' hats shall be quite plain, with a black flat loop and button. The Officers will wear white stocks, and the regimental boots are to be fastened to the back part of the knee of the breeches by a black strap and buckle."

1788. *March* 17.—The annual issues of clothing were settled by the Master-General as follows:—

Each sergeant to receive annually—

    1 coat.
    1 white cloth waistcoat.

1 pair of shoe-brushes.
1 cloth brush.
1 twin screw and worm.
1 brush and pricker.
1 leather stock.
1 rosette.
1 pair of knee-buckles.
1 stock-buckle.
1 large and 1 small comb.

    (Duncan's "History R.A.")

ARTILLERY DRIVER, CIRCA 1785.

PLATE IX.

A GUNNER OF THE ROYAL ARTILLERY.

1797.

DESCRIPTION OF PLATE.

THE gunner of this period wore two cross-belts; one carried the bayonet, and the other the pouch. On the front of the one carrying the pouch was a hammer and pair of prickers for the vent of the gun.

A crimson cord ran along the centre of the belt, and from this depended a small powder-horn for priming the vent.

AUTHORITIES.—Coloured print, title, "Present Arms—First Motion." 1797.
Orders for dress as quoted in text.

1 pair white cloth breeches.
1 frilled shirt.
1 black leather stock.
1 pair of worsted stockings.

1 gold-laced hat.
Black cloth, with 3 dozen buttons for—
1 pair of gaiters.
5s. 3d. in lieu of a pair of shoes.

The same articles were supplied to the other ranks, with the exception that, while the corporal's coat had two epaulettes, the bombardier's had only one, and that the hats of the drummers were plain instead of gold-laced. The drummers had also fur caps supplied to them when required. In the West Indies the men received white linen waistcoats and breeches, instead of cloth; and wore white gold-laced hats instead of black.

The men of the Invalid Battalion received the same articles as those of the Marching Battalions, with this exception: that their coats were lined with *red* instead of white, and their waistcoats and breeches, instead of being white, were *blue*.

(Duncan's "History R.A.")

1791. *July* 5.—Two epaulettes ordered to be worn upon the General Officers' frock uniform, in like manner as upon the great uniform; and the Field Officers to be distinguished by also wearing an epaulette on each shoulder. (Kane's List.)

1793. For description of uniform of R.H.A. and R.A., see General Mercer's MS. Notes, p. 49, *et seq*.

1794. *August* 8.—Garrison Orders by Lieut.-Colonel Farrington:—

ARTILLERY DRIVER, 1792.

"The Officers lately appointed are informed that the regimental waistcoats are without flaps, and with one row of buttons only, the same as the men's. The breeches, which are cloth or

PLATE X.

AN OFFICER AND GUNNER, ROYAL ARTILLERY.

1799.

Description of Plate.

The gunner is presenting arms to a Field Officer of this date.

The gunners had left off the long-tailed coats, and taken into wear single-breasted, short-tailed ones. It will be noticed that the Officer had an entirely different style of coat to that worn in Plate No. 8. It was double breasted, and the sword was carried depending from a shoulder-belt.

Authorities.—Coloured print, "Officer R.A.," in the "British Military Library." 1799.
    Portrait of Lieut.-General Congreve, R.A.
    Miniature of an Officer R.A.
    Water-colour sketches in "Artillery Movements," MS. drill-book. 1799.

GEORGE III.

kerseymere, are likewise the same as the men's, and buckle at the knee. The tops of the boots are bound and lined with white leather, and buckle up with a black strap. The sword has a straight blade, and the length of it as established by his Majesty's regulations; it is to be worn with a crimson-and-gold sword-knot. The lappels of the coat are buttoned back and hooked together, and the skirts hooked up."

1796. *October* 12.—General Orders:—

"The Officers of Artillery are to conform to the uniform hat and sword, as established by his Majesty for the Army."

October 30.—General Orders:—

"The Master-General is extremely willing to comply with the wishes of the Colonels Commandant, and desires they will fix upon a cross-belt and plate for the sword, which may be uniform with that worn in the Army."

1797. *November* 6.—General Orders:—

"The Officers to wear white feathers in their hats, similar in appearance to the men's."

1798. *July* 5.—General Orders:—

"His Majesty's Order of the 26th May, respecting the dress of the Officers of the Line, are to be considered to be extended to the Officers of Artillery. The Officers' sashes, in conformity thereto, to be worn over the coat."

1799. *Uniform of the Officers.*—Blue faced with scarlet, gold epaulettes, no lace, white waistcoat and breeches, boots, yellow breast-plate, on white buff shoulder-belt.

Uniform of the Privates.—Blue, with red cuffs and collar, no facings, yellow lace and buttons, impressed with the ordnance arms.

The sergeants wear gold lace frogged.

Arms.—Sergeants: swords yellow-hilted. Corporals, bombardiers, and privates: carbine and bayonet. Horse Artillery: sword and pistols.

(The "British Military Library," 1799.)

SIXTH BATTALION, RAISED 1799.—The following was the dress of the battalion at its formation in 1799, as also of the whole regiment except Horse Artillery:—

The Officers wore blue cloth double-breasted coats, with scarlet lappels; the Field Officers had two epaulettes, the Company Officers only one, which they wore on the right shoulder; white kerseymere breeches; long black leather boots, fastened to the

PLATE XI.

AN OFFICER OF THE ROYAL HORSE ARTILLERY.

1815.

DESCRIPTION OF PLATE.

THIS represents the uniform worn during the Waterloo epoch for home service, as overalls worn over boots and breeches were usually the kit on foreign and active service. *Vide* Plate XII.

The Officers wore their sword-belts under the jacket, and attached to the sword by slings. It is interesting to compare this plate with No. 7, and to notice the difference between the jackets.

Very large blue shabracques with tassels, and stiffened with leather at the ends, were used.

AUTHORITIES.—Coloured print from Goddard's "Armies of Europe." 1812.
 Coloured print from "The Picturesque Representation of the Dress and Manners of the English." 1814.
 Coloured print from Beamish's "History of the King's German Legion." 1814.
 Coloured print from Hamilton Smith's "Military Costume of the British Empire."

GEORGE III.

back part of the knee of the breeches by a black strap and buckle; and a cocked hat, with gold loop and button and white feather.

The non-commissioned officers and men wore blue cloth coats, single breasted, laced in front and on the cuffs and flaps, the staff-sergeants and sergeants with gold lace, and the rank and file with yellow worsted lace.

The staff-sergeants wore two gold bullion epaulettes; the sergeants two gold-laced straps; the corporals two fringe epaulettes; the bombardiers one fringe epaulette on the right shoulder; the gunners two worsted straps.

(Duncan's "History R.A.," vol. i.)

The changes in uniform during this period (1800-1812) were not so marked as to make it necessary to show them in a coloured plate.

1803.—By General Orders of October 31 and November 1, 1803, the Officers, non-commissioned officers, and men of the various companies which had served in Egypt, were permitted to wear the "Sphynx," with the word "Egypt," on their regimental caps; but the distinction was a *personal* one, and not to be perpetuated in the companies. (Duncan's "History R.A.")

1803. *December* 29.—General Orders:—

"The Master-General permits Officers of Artillery to wear blue pantaloons and boots in the field; and considering the possibility, at this particular period, of Officers being suddenly called into the field, permits blue pantaloons and boots to be worn in garrison, expect upon guard, under arms, or any dressed parade."

ARTILLERY DRIVER, 1799.

1805. *February* 10.—General Orders:—

"The feathers in the caps of the corporals, bombardiers, and gunners, are not to exceed ten inches in height; the feathers of the Officers, staff-sergeants, and sergeants are not to exceed thirteen inches."

PLATE XII.

TROOPER IN THE MOUNTED ROCKET CORPS OF THE ROYAL HORSE ARTILLERY.

1815.

DESCRIPTION OF PLATE.

THIS plate shows a trooper of the Rocket Corps: he is wearing the overalls, always worn on active service; they are buttoned on over his boots and breeches, and are chained down under the feet. His arms consist of a pistol and sabre, the latter being held in a frog, which was attached to the saddle.

The shabracque is stiffened with leather to keep it stretched.

AUTHORITIES.—Coloured plate from Congreve's "Rocket System." 1814.
　Two coloured prints, titles, "Artilleur Anglaise." Circa 1812.
　Coloured print from Hamilton Smith's "Military Costume of the British Empire." 1815.

GEORGE III.

1806. *November* 1.—General Orders (dress of Officers R.H.A.):—

"Except at dress parades, the blue regimental overalls are to be worn till dinner-time in place of the blue pantaloons, which is to be the afternoon dress when at home.

"At all parades, whether mounted or dismounted, and during the day, the black velvet stock is to be worn, with an inch of shirt-collar over it; no other white to be shown.

"In the evenings it is requested that black silk handkerchiefs may be substituted, with the same proportion of shirt-collar over them.

"When Officers are dressed for a ball, evening party, or dine out, they are to wear the jacket open, white pantaloons, plain white waistcoat (with sash over it), light sword, regulation sword-knot, black belt, with cocked hat and feather.

"In common a white leather sword-knot is to be worn. Spurs with horizontal rowels to be worn at all times."

1807. *November* 29. — General Orders :—

"The Officers' great-coats, of the Marching Battalions, are to be plain blue cloth, with a single row of flat metal buttons."

1808. *April* 10.—General Orders:—

"There is to be no difference in the length of the feather worn by the Officers, non-commissioned officers, and gunners of the Marching Battalions."

GUNNER R.A., 1806.

DRIVER CORPS, 1806.

August 1.—His Majesty's Orders for the Army to dispense with the use of queues, were directed by the Master-General to be extended to the Artillery. The Commanding Officers of regiments were directed to take care that the men's hair be cut close in their necks, in the neatest and most uniform manner, and that their heads

---

AUTHORITIES 1800-1812. — Coloured print, "The French Invasion; or, Buonaparte landing in Great Britain." Published by H. Humphreys. 1803.

Two Coloured prints, "Atkinson's Picturesque Costume of Great Britain." T. A. Atkinson, del. Published by W. Miller. 1807.

Two Coloured prints, "Royal British Artillery" — Goddard's "Armies of Europe." Published by Goddard. 1812.

PLATE XIII.

AN OFFICER AND GUNNER, ROYAL ARTILLERY.

1815.

DESCRIPTION OF PLATE.

THE Officer in the foreground is wearing the full-dress coatee of the period, white breeches, and Hessian boots.

This coatee is quite unique, and was worn for a very short time. The felt cap is a distinct feature of the Waterloo epoch. The dress of this period is decidedly a handsome one.

AUTHORITIES.—Full-dress coatee in R.A.I. Circa 1812.
　　　Portrait of Colonel Percy Drummond, R.A. Circa 1815.
　　　Engravings from Booth's "History of the Battle of Waterloo." 1815.
　　　Coloured print from Beamish's "History of the King's German Legion." 1814.
　　　Coloured print from Hamilton Smith's "Military Costume of the British Empire." 1815.

GEORGE III.

be kept perfectly clean, by combing, brushing, and frequently washing them; for the latter essential purpose, a small sponge was ordered to be added to each man's regimental necessaries. (Kane's List.)

1810. *January* 24.—General Orders :—

"Care is to be taken that the gaiters are of sufficient length to reach the knee-pan, the tops to be cut perfectly straight, and no button to be put behind. No part of the waistcoat is to be seen, and the jacket is to come well down, so as to cover the upper part of the breeches. The skirt is to be the same as furnished by the contractor, 9 inches in length."

March 2.—Field Officers, whether by brevet or otherwise, were directed to wear two epaulettes; the epaulettes worn by Field Officers and Captains to be of bullion, those by the Subaltern Officers of fringe. (Kane's List.)

1811. *July.*—General Orders :—

"By command of His Royal Highness, the Prince Regent, the Master-General of the Ordnance will in future wear a blue uniform, with scarlet facing and gold embroidery, made up according to the pattern of the established uniform of a General in His Majesty's Service.

"The Lieut.-General of the Ordnance will in future wear a blue uniform, with scarlet facings, and gold embroidery, made up according to the pattern of the established uniform of a Lieut.-General in His Majesty's Service.

"The Deputy Adjutant-General of Artillery will in future wear a blue uniform, with scarlet facings and silver embroidery, made up according to the pattern of the established uniform of a Major-General in His Majesty's Service."

1812. *January* 14.—General Orders :—

"The Officers of the Horse Artillery are to wear jackets similar to the private men, with an aiguilette.

"In parade dress, they are to wear white leather pantaloons and Hussar boots, with gold binding.

"On ordinary duties, or on a march, they are to wear overalls, of a colour similar to the private men's, and a short surtout, which is calculated to be worn likewise as a pelisse on service.

"When attending a drawing-room, or *levée*, they may appear in long coats, with lappels and aiguilettes, the same as are worn with the jacket, but without lace on the seams; or in the regimental jacket, as they may prefer.

ARTILLERY DRIVER, 1810–1815.

48   HISTORY OF THE DRESS OF THE ROYAL ARTILLERY.

"The Officers of the Horse Artillery are likewise to wear cocked hats, with the star loop, with the dress regimentals.

"Officers of the Battalions of Artillery are to wear a cap of a pattern similar to the private men's; a regimental coat similar to the private men's, with lace, but with lappels to button over the breast and body, with white pantaloons and half-boots; a grey cloth great-coat, corresponding in colour with that established for the men.

"In the case of companies employed on foreign service, the Officers are to wear grey pantaloons or overalls, with short boots, or with shoes and gaiters, such as the private men's.

"The Field and Staff Officers of Battalions are to conform to the aforegoing regulations, the same as Officers of Companies.

"When at Court, the Officers are to appear in long coats, embroidered according to the pattern, with cocked hats as at present."

July 31.—General Order :—

"The lace round the rim of the front of the Officer's cap is to be taken off, and the front to be bound with black silk ferret."

August 12.—The triangular ornament, similar to that of the men's, is to be worn upon the Officers' embroidered jacket. (Kane's List.)

1813.   *August* 3.—General Orders :—

"The bottom of the fringe of the lower or longest tassel to be 1 inch from the extreme bottom of the cap, and the bottom of the upper or shortest tassel to be 2 inches from the extreme bottom of the cap, and each of the tassels to be sewn to the cap, three-quarters of an inch above the head of the tassel, to prevent them swinging about.

"Officers of R.H.A. to wear the triangular ornament on the embroidered jacket, similar to that worn by the men.

OFFICER OF FOOT ARTILLERY, 1812.

"The cocked hat worn by staff-sergeants, and the cap of sugar-loaf shape worn by other non-commissioned officers and men, discontinued. A cap with a low crown, and false stand-up collar of a Belgian fashion, with cord and tassel, worn by Officers and men. A colour-sergeant sanctioned for each company, to be distinguished by a badge of a regimental colour above the chevrons, supported by two crossed swords (*July* 6)."

1816. The Belgic cap abolished, and a broad-crowned chako with black lacquered leather top introduced, having a peak before and behind; the latter proved so unsightly and inconvenient that it was ordered, a few weeks later, to be cut off. This chako was

GEORGE III.

trimmed with gold lace at the top and bottom. Companies on the continent, in America, and in garrison abroad, were supplied with blue-grey trousers and gaiters, instead of breeches and black gaiters.

The end of the eighteenth and the beginning of the nineteenth centuries form a period of very great interest to soldiers in general, and the Royal Regiment of Artillery in particular. Details as to dress, drill, manners, and customs of this period are very hard to obtain, and are therefore all the more valuable when related by one living and serving in the Artillery during this time. I have, therefore, taken the liberty of giving *in extenso* the MS. notes, and thumb-nail sketches written and drawn in 1840 by the late General A. C. Mercer, No. 1064, Kane's List, Colonel Commandant of the 9th Brigade—the Captain Mercer of Waterloo fame.

These MS. notes contain an account of the first formation of a troop of Horse Artillery, and give a description of the uniform first worn by the Royal Horse Artillery, and from which description I have drawn plate No. 8, also an account of the drills, etc., of the Artillery. These MS. notes were lent to me by General T. W. Mercer, and it is by his kind permission that I am now able to publish them.

ARTILLERY DRIVER, 1815–1822.

MILITARY REMINISCENCES OF LATTER END OF EIGHTEENTH AND BEGINNING OF NINETEENTH CENTURIES.

By General A. C. Mercer, R.A.

Many are the insignificant trifles which, associated as they are with times gone by, I would not wish to let slip, and therefore throw them together while still living in my mind's eye.

1789. Dress. *Hair-clubs.*—My first and earliest recollections on this subject present to me the soldiers of the 8th and 12th Regiments (successively quartered in the Island of Guernsey, in or about the year 1789 or '90), dressing each other's heads under a lamp in one of the bastions of Fort George. The operation was to plaster well with grease, whiten with flour, and to roll the hair behind in a club, which was effected by means of an iron something of the sort as here shown.

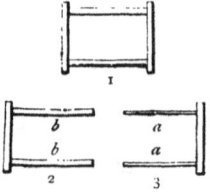

The hair was rolled up on No. 1, and when the club was made, the instrument was removed by drawing it out sideways, the branches *a, a* of No. 3 fitting into the pipes *b, b* of No. 2. The club, when completed, was nearly of the annexed form.

It was fastened by a black leather band, *a*, ornamented with a rosette. The whole was made as white as a cauliflower.

1794. *Queues.*—My next recollection on this subject was at Plymouth, in 1794, when the Officers wore small queues tied with a few turns of riband, and ornamented with a rather large silk rosette. What the men wore, I now forget; but all were still powdered. My own experience gave me the next occasion to notice military friseurship when, in the beginning of 1798, I went to the Royal Academy at Woolwich, and the doctoring my head underwent at that time will give the fashion of the day. On the top the hair was cut close, and the stumps well rubbed back with hard or stick pomatum, a kind of grease made up in hard rolls about an inch in diameter, and three or four inches long, if I recollect right, run into paper moulds, like resin for the violin. The stumpy hair, at first stubborn, by perseverance

and pomatum, was after a time quite forced out of its natural direction, and made to grow backwards instead of forwards. The remainder of the hair was gathered into a queue behind, which, according to regulation, should be 10 inches long, and tied close to the head; this we called a rooter, but the dandies affected a loose tye, and began some inches lower down. Those whose hair was not long enough had false queues made of stuffed chamois leather with a brush of hair at the end, and this had to be spliced on to his own hair. For uniformity sake, the gunners, etc., wore false queues of strong black leather, which they cleaned and polished like their shoes.

As it was difficult to tie one's own queue, we used to assist each other, and it was a sort of accomplishment, the being able to give a good queue. But the visits of two barbers once a fortnight offered the best opportunity of getting a capital queue—

sometimes, to be sure, such a rooter that it was difficult to shut the eyes; yet many slept in them for a whole week, or till the next barberian visit.

A stiff rosette of polished leather was stuck on by a brass hook that went into the queue, which was a hollow pipe. Annexed is some idea of them.

At the time we went to church in the old Repository, greasing and whitening the head was in full go, and never shall I forget the stench emanating from so many filthy heads crowded together in the low rooms where service was performed—of course, more particularly in hot weather. The lines round the queue were, I imagine, made to represent the winding of the riband. The hair of the sides and back of the head having been well greased with soft pomatum (more or less scented) made of hog's lard, the whole was thoroughly dusted with hair-powder, combed through again and again until brought to an even appearance.

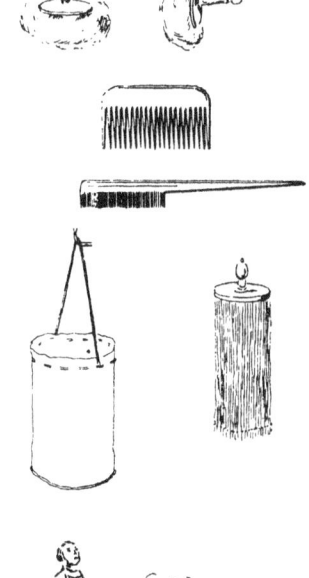

Lord! what funny things our dressing-boxes were in those days! A tray on the top to hold combs and hard pomatum, small boxes for the soft below, and two large ones like sugar-boxes for powder, in which was the puff made of down. These boxes were generally made of tin and lacquered brown. The mysteries of the toilette were manifold in those days. Of combs there were multitudes; I remember only the rack, the ordinary comb, and the curling comb. N.B.—A pair of curling-irons usually formed part of the contents of a box. Ladies, besides the common puff of down, used another as a finisher. This was made of silk, forming a kind of tassel of long cords, and the operator, in using it, always stood at the distance of two or three feet from the poudree, and darted the powder at the head by catching the blow aimed at the head with the right hand, on the left wrist, which jerked the powder out of the silken puff and gave it an impulse toward the already-saturated head, where it settled down in beautiful impalpability. White was not the only powder used; there was another of a pale cinnamon colour, called brown-powder, or more fashionable "Marechale." The peculiar uses of this I forget, or never knew, probably because it was peculiarly a lady's powder. How well I remember standing by my mother's toilet, eyeing with

curiosity all the varied combings and curlings and powderings, as she sat wrapped in her flannel dressing-gown! and when all was done then came the powder-knife (another indispensable in the dressing-box), with which the powder was carefully removed from the face without disturbing the hair. This knife was a flat piece of iron set in a tortoise-shell handle, double-edged, but not sharp, very like a spatula on a small scale. The great stock-in-trade of a perfumer in those days was hair-powder of sorts, brown and white, of all possible odours—I think the favourite was violet; next pomatums, equally varying in fragrance, smartly done up in bluish-white gallipots, more or less ornamented, and with an ornamental paper cover. The powder was made up in paper bags of pound and half-pound each. Our allowance at the Academy used to be 1½ lb. per month to each cadet, and a pot of pomatum; hard ditto when wanted, which was not often. The day of serving out the powder was generally marked by one or more battles in front of the barracks, where pounds or half-pounds were pelted about like snow-balls—a delightful amusement, for nothing could exceed the fun of bursting one of these projectiles against a fellow's face, and the smoke caused by such numerous explosions was so like that of a real battle. The whitened trunks of the trees, and the great splashes on the dingy red-brick front of the barracks, bore testimony for many a day to the hotness of the fight.

But I am digressing. The subsequent modifications of the queues and tops I forget the dates of. The thick ten-inch queue of the Officers (those of the men were never altered) gave way to long thin ones made of whalebone; and instead of the old rosette, the enveloping riband terminated at the upper part in a most elaborately flowing bunch, which fluttered about one on a windy day like so many black streamers. Dandies (who, of course, are dandies because in extremes) affected something monstrous in this way; and although the queue itself had now increased in length until the tuft at the lower end was as low as the waist (the natural one, I mean, for that arranged by the tailors was, about this period, almost under the arms), and its thickness only that of a quill, the flies of riband hung much lower when in a state of rest, and streamed out to an immense distance in the wind. The present Sir John Conroy (of Court notoriety) was an amazing dandy, and that unfortunate fellow Green (who was in the same troop with him, and quite as great a dandy) used to say that if Conroy was coming down a street before the wind, you might have notice of his

approach a quarter of an hour before his person appeared, by the streams of riband fluttering before him.

About this time queues were no longer attempted even to be imposed on the public as real, by attaching them to one's own hair. They were tied round the neck, between the white cravat and black stock which was worn over it, and although then so accustomed to the sight as not to notice it, yet in 1840 people's cachinnatory muscles would be set in motion, no doubt, by seeing a man's head turning right and left whilst his supposed hair hung unmoved.

The business of hairdressing was pushed to a ridiculous excess by the late Duke of Kent, particularly whilst Governor of Gibraltar. The first person who boarded every ship coming into harbour was His Royal Highness's hairdresser, and no officer was allowed to land until he had submitted his head to be operated on by this functionary. On the top it was to be cut in a horseshoe form; a string put round the ear and held in the mouth, decided the termination (downwards) of the whiskers; and such fooleries. Sir A. Frazer once travelled in a coach with a wild-looking boy of sixteen, whose hair was as shaggy as that of a wild colt. He was going then to join the Duke's Regiment, whence he had been sent, with six months' leave of absence and positive orders not to cut his hair, which on his first joining had been found too short to admit of being properly put into shape. The 1st Royals long retained their queues after every other regiment had discarded them, and, after all, may be said to have been taken from them by force, the general officer commanding (at Wheely Malder or Danbury Borray, I forget which) having threatened to have them cut off on parade unless removed by a specified day. Meanwhile courier upon courier was said to have passed between the Commanding Officer of the regiment and Kensington Palace, where His Royal Highness then lived. Alas, poor queues!

The exact year when powder and queues expired, I don't exactly remember. It appears to me that the death-blow was given by the earlier Peninsular campaigns, but there are other things that stagger me in this belief. I remember, for instance, powdering the side locks after putting my helmet on in 1808, and wearing queues in 1809–10, etc. Yet do I also remember, in 1802 or 1803, at Cork on some occasion of rejoicing, that our colonel (Howorth) ordered the party which paraded to fire a salute on the quay at George Island, to powder, and I also remember the impression on my mind made by their appearance with white heads, which I thought very ridiculous, which would not have been the case had my eye been accustomed to it. Further, I remember how conceited I was about my own brown hair (which certainly was luxuriant and beautifully curling), and how certain ladies, whose pet I was, taught me to brush and anoint it with Huile Antique, then the fashionable application; and it was this conceit and preference to a brown head that made me, as I have stated above, powder my side locks, after putting my helmet on, so keeping the rest clean, which shows that it was still necessary to appear powdered at parade in 1808. And I remember, also, that it was as necessary in going to mess, there being a fine for any one going to dinner without —a most cogent reason for my dining so often in my room, as I did whilst at Woolwich that year.

All this induces me to believe that powder was left off by the men much earlier than by the Officers, and that queues were worn by both long after powder had ceased among the men. In Kane's book I find the order for discontinuing queues is dated August 1st, 1808, for the Ordnance Corps, but Sir Augustus (then Captain) Frazer made us leave queues and feathers behind in 1807, when we went to the Rio de la Plata. Still the Master-General's order for providing the men with spunges to wash their heads, etc., looks as if they had powdered up to that time. In civil life, every one must remember Lord Matthew, afterwards Lord Llandaff, remarkable at once for his large and commanding figure, and retaining his queue and powder long after it had disappeared everywhere else.

Coiffure.—The first head-dress I remember as worn by the Royal Artillery was at Plymouth, 1794 or 1795. That of the non-commissioned officers and gunners was what would now be considered very ridiculous. How others might have considered  it at that epoch I cannot decide, but that in my eyes it was exceeding smart is undeniable. It was a round hat of the true Mother Shipton breed. Narrow (very narrow) brim, very high crown, going smaller upwards, so that it formed a frustum of an acute cone. This elegant coiffure was orna-  mented with a broad yellow band, and a cockade in front of the roof, surmounted by a scarlet tuft. The hat worn by the Officers at the same period would not even now be considered ungraceful—round, with a brim somewhat broad, and curling up at the sides; low, rounded crown, over all a bearskin in the helmet fashion, cockade, and I think a white feather in the left side—of this last not quite sure. When this was changed for the cocked hat I am also uncertain, but think it must have been about 1797, or perhaps earlier, for in Kane's book there is an order of October 12th, 1796, that the Artillery shall conform to the regulation hat and

GEORGE III.

sword, etc., and when I first went to Woolwich, latter end of 1797, I remember seeing all the men in cocked hats.

Horrid ugly things they were, too, especially the men's, made of very coarse felt, and heavy as lead; they turned upwards, instead of drooping, as was afterwards considered the criterion of beauty. Just fitting on the crown of the head, the slightest breeze sufficed to uncover a whole regiment, had it not been for weight and a small string made into a loop, both ends of which being attached to the hat, the bend was passed under the hair behind; so that, on going into church, the men had rather an awkward operation to perform ere they could uncover. When I got my first commission, not having the slightest idea of the points constituting beauty in a cocked hat, I went to Wagner, in Pall Mall, simply ordered a hat and feather according to the regulations; and until I found myself the laughing-stock of all my companions at the first guard-mounting parade, had no suspicion that such a respectable house would have taken in a boy, by palming on him that which no one else would ever have taken off their hands. In a word, it was large, ungainly, and—horror of horrors!—the sides curled upward, like the gunners', whereas the droop had just begun to be all the go. Moreover, the conical feather, though strictly of the regimental length, etc., was like nobody else's, and hideous. I shall never forget my first hat and feather.

The Infantry hat was decorated by a crimson-and-gold rosette in each lock. The cavalry by a pendant tassel of the same material. This, of course, we aped whenever we dared.

The regulation mode of wearing this hat was with the loop, etc., perpendicularly over the left eye, and the right corner, or wing, thrown a little forward. What might be termed right shoulders forward. Some of the old men still adhered as nearly as the regulations would admit, to the form of their antique Dettingen hats—triangular. The Navy, instead of wearing their cocked hats square over the brow, like the soldiers, slewed them round, bringing the ends off, as they call it, "fore and aft." This the Army soon began to imitate, when off parade, and many a youngster got toko for being caught with his beaver in this unlawful fix.

I think it must have been about 1810, 1811, or 1812, that general Officers wore feathered hats in imitation of the French. The fashion did not last many years.

The relaxation admitted on actual service, however, was always taken advantage of to get rid of the feather and the square position of the hat, so that, from seeing  people returning from expeditions with their hats fore and aft, an idea of service got to be associated with this form of wearing it, wonderfully taking, particularly with the young aspirants for glory, and by them communicated to the women, who soon learned to look on a man as a spiritless quiz, who stuck to regulation in wearing his uniform. Somehow or another, this fashion in the end has completely gained the ascendency, and the present wearers of hats (Staff and Engineers) never dream of bringing the loop perpendicularly over the left eye. Like every other article of clothing, the hat has continually varied its shape within my day. The original cocked hat was triangular, as may be seen in old portraits of the  Duke of Cumberland, General Elliot, General Wolfe, and a host of others; then came the broader brim, which made the cocks longer and fan higher, but with the base line straight, or even inclining upwards. An improvement on this was the droop as exhibited in the last sketch. But dandies, as I said,  are dandies by running everything into extremes—*in extremum* are. The droop, once suggested, was gradually increased until, when square, the rosettes interfered with a man's shoulders; when fore and aft, the foremost part hid the face, and the hinder served instead of a "hand" to scratch between the shoulders behind. Still, the fan was high. By-and-by, *id est*, about 1805 I think, low fans (or lower) became the fashion, which recalls to me what a conceited little puppy I was, when the Cavalry and Horse Artillery adopted the cocked hat as an undress, which was worn with the pelisse. Mine, I remember, was one of the low fans, with the spunge-head feather. What a jackanapes I must have been, caracoling about Stephen's Green and Merrion Square, in the little, ugly, poor  pelisse of yon day with this selfsame hideous hat!

After the peace of 1815, the high acute fan obtained generally, and still holds its ground. Thenceforward I think the fan, and, indeed, the  general bulk of the hat, gradually diminished until 1815, when imitation of the French had begun to make it look up again. The acme of *petitesse* was, I believe, attained by the immortal Wellington, whose funny little hat is now familiar to all the world.

Feathers naturally follow hats; their fashion has been as variable, and may be briefly stated. I have already said that I forget whether any feather was worn in the bearskin hat—the earliest of recollections. When I joined the Royal Artillery, the ugliest thing ever devised by tasteless adjutants was stuck up in our hats, a conical white feather, about six inches high, and stiff as it could be. How long this lasted I know not, but its successor was an incumbrance—ten inches long, the top spreading out in long hackles, stiff stem; this was improved after a time by having the whalebone weaker, so that instead of standing bolt upright, the feather (still of the same make and dimensions) drooped gracefully (as it was thought) over the fan of the hat. How such hideous incumbrances could ever have been devised I cannot imagine, and thought the ridiculous had reached the extreme until the absurd, horrible, preposterous, tasteless mountain of feathers worn by our Hussars and Staff of enlightened *aujourd'hui*, met my astonished gaze. Then, indeed, I did wonder!

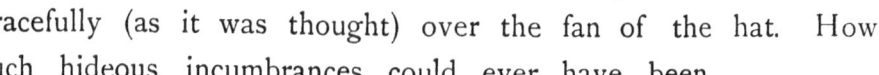

A YOUNGSTER OF 1800.

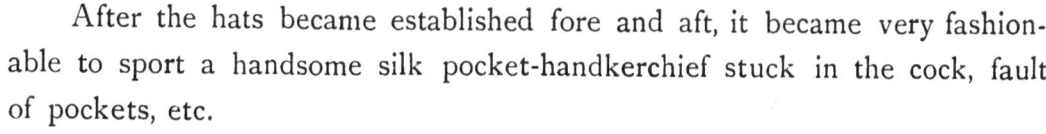

After the hats became established fore and aft, it became very fashionable to sport a handsome silk pocket-handkerchief stuck in the cock, fault of pockets, etc.

Helmets, etc.—The first head-dress of the Horse Artillery was a helmet—the old English Light Dragoon helmet (helmets with green turbans were always worn by Light Infantry companies), the favourite of George III.; the handsomest, most military, and most serviceable of all military coiffures; the admiration of all foreigners, and the only article truly national ever worn in the British Army. Vain were the attempts of His Royal Highness the Prince of Wales, of Lord Paget, of the Duke of Cumberland, and of Sir Charles Stuart, to get rid of the helmet, and denationalizing the 10th, 7th, 15th, and 18th Light Dragoons to make Hussars of them; so long as old George lived, or at least retained his reason, the helmet he would never allow to be changed. The good old man was aware of all its excellences, and he loved it as a truly national costume. With our venerable Sovereign disappeared the helmet from every corps in the Army. Light Dragoons as well as Hussars, excepting the Horse Artillery, who, spite of modern dandyism, retained it until very recently—I believe 1835, or thereabouts—when, under the reign of a Hussar Master-General, Whinyates, Dunn, Michell, *cum multis aliis*, who, instead of feeling pride at being distinguished as Horse Artillery *sui generis*, longed to become Hussars themselves, at last succeeded in banishing the helmet, and with it every particle of dress, and perhaps feeling, that once distinguished the corps from, and elevated above, every other in the Army. Like the cocked hat, the helmet in the course of years varied in ornament and form, and although essentially the same, yet latterly was a very different, and far more elegant article of dress than when I first saw it in 1797. Here I confess in one point to be uncertain—I mean as to the nature of the turban or ornamental fillet, surrounding the lower part; but I think it was of leopard-skin similar to the helmets of the Light Dragoons. This, however, could not have lasted long, for my first distinct recollection is of a crimson silk turban. On or about 1805, we succeeded, through the medium of Lady Chatham (his lordship was Master-General), in getting turbans of black velvet; for all the Light Dragoons wore black silk turbans, and, alas! even in those days the mania for imitating the Cavalry existed. The drivers (or Wee Gee Corps) had dark-blue

HELMET OF 1799.

turbans, which was a sad nuisance to us, so nearly resembling our own, that another change was obtained in a few months, to black silk, which delighted us all, for the Cavalry wore black silk. This might have been about the latter part of 1805, or beginning of 1806, and afterwards no alteration took place until their abolition. The form of the helmet formerly was very ugly, straight line at bottom, with the shade or peak sticking straight out, and very large. The bearskin low and poor.

By degrees all this was changed, until, from an ugly, it became really an elegant article of dress. Like the cocked hat, one of its principal improvements consisted in an alteration of the base line from straight to curved, which, with the shade, made it droop over the face in front, and into the neck behind, thus at once improving its

appearance and its qualities as a defence for the knowledge-box. At the same time, the bearskins were raised and made fuller.

The first time this was done for the non-commissioned officers and men, I remember, we made the alteration ourselves (*i.e.* our collar-maker did it) by uniting the bearskin of the old helmet to the new one just served out, and a monstrous improvement it made in the appearance of our parades. There is

nothing like a lofty head-dress to make soldiers look imposing, particularly so when drawn up in a body. The feathers worn in the helmets of officers differed like those for the cocked hats; those of the men, I believe, were always the same, for the feather-case was always of the same form and dimensions. The helmet was latterly decorated, and perhaps rendered more perfect, by gilt scales attached to the sides. When not worn down, these were turned to and tied in rear of the bearskin.

Forage-caps.—The most ungraceful head-dress that could well be devised, I think, was the fatigue-cap worn by the Foot Artillery when I first entered the regiment, and only required the combination with the loose canvas frock and waistcoat to make it

hideously unmilitary. It was of black leather, with a brass ornament in front (G.R. and crown, etc.), the leather not stiff, full of cracks, and looking rusty, for they were never cleaned or expected to be. The Horse Artillery and drivers had a similar mitre-shaped cap, but better, inasmuch as, being made of thick stiff leather, it was kept polished, and looked smart. This was used for undress parades, watering order, etc. But for common stable parades, fatigues, etc., the Horse Artillery had a blue cloth cap edged with red, and tied behind with red ferreting. This was also worn at night by stable sentries and others.

The captains of troops must have been greater men, and have enjoyed much more latitude formerly, than in the present day. Many circumstances which I call to mind make me think this, but among other, the circumstance that Duncan, in 1804, took it into his head to give his troop a new and Frenchified forage-cap, such an one as until then was only known to us through the medium of costumes, etc., although familiar to him, a service officer. Numerous were the fancies he and I tried, some in sketches, some he actually had made up, until at last we pitched upon the annexed as the most elegant; and the tailors were forthwith set to work making them up.

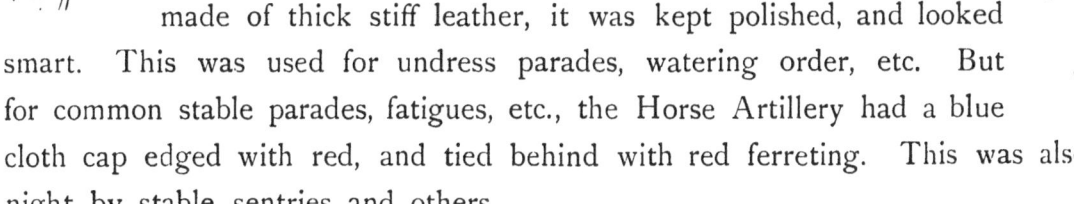

In a short time they were finished, Duncan delighted; inspected the watering-order parade himself, and contemplated the beautiful effect of his Frenchified troop with rapture. It was marched off, and again he took his stand at the end of the lane by which (*en route* for the Phœnix Park) they must gain the street of Island Bridge. The last of them had scarcely passed the bridge when, issuing from the barracks appeared the drivers, also in watering-order. But, oh horror! carefully as the intended change had been concealed, and carefully as had the intended pattern been guarded, old Colonel Schalch had managed to ferret it out, and there went the Wee Gees bridling in their finery, to the disgust of Duncan, whose rage I shall long remember. These caps, or something similar, were afterwards adopted generally, and here let me confess my uncertainty whether the 16th Light Dragoons, or the 12th or both, had not these caps before us.

(In those days there was no undress-cap for officers, ergo when off parade they were usually lounging about in round hats, and in some small or slack garrisons I have seen them walking about the streets in them. In the Foot Artillery, at some of our outquarters, we always wore them, with a cockade and button, as substitutes for cocked hats. In the West Indies, I think, they were worn by authority.)

Coats, Jackets, etc.—From the chief, descending to the middle man and taxing my memory as to its earliest impressions in or about 1795, I remember the gay young  officers of Artillery sporting about the streets or dock at Plymouth in blue coats with red facings buttoned back, hooked at the collar, and falling off as they descended, so as to show the white kerseymere waistcoat. Whether the skirts were sewn or hooked back, I cannot remember, but believe the former. A single epaulet decorated this coat, on the right shoulder of captains and lieutenants; field-officers alone wearing two. To these coats succeeded the double-breasted one, equally plain with the other, which was sometimes worn closely buttoned up; but more generally (and I think such was the order) the three upper buttons undone and the lappels turned back, with the cambric shirt-frill pulled out in the form of a cock's comb. Still no lace, no ornament, save the epaulet. I remember at Clonmel, in 1802, venturing (out of the world, as we then considered ourselves) to stick grenades in our skirts, and thus decorated fancying ourselves uncommonly fine fellows, as we figured away at the balls in the Court-house. After this, I know nothing further of the Foot Artillery, except that their uniform underwent several changes, from coat to jacket, etc. The first lace (beside the epaulet) was an embroidered true lover's knot upon red cloth, as a skirt ornament; then they got cord lace and embroidery—always something very tasteless and ugly. At one time they had no less than five different coats or jackets. The Horse Artillery, which I joined in 1804, wore flat lace on their jackets, although the Light Dragoons had been wearing the cord lace for some years. The regulation jacket was to have on the breast equal blue and lace, that is, the space between the lace was to be of the same breadth as the lace itself. This, however, was too poor to satisfy us; and as regulations in those days were little adhered to away from headquarters, every one put on as much more lace as his fancy dictated or his purse permitted. For my part, my first jacket resembled a furze-bush in full blossom, for it was one mass of gold from the collar to the sash. No great space, after all, for the waists were then worn so exceedingly short that my sash was nearly under my arms; and other jackets which I had afterwards, of more modest description, had only six loops of lace on the breast. It was the fashion of the day for boys to imitate or try to resemble women, wearing as they did such short waists, and filling out the jacket with handkerchiefs to resemble the female figure. Yet, with all this, it strikes me that the youngsters then, in spite of their feminine appearance, were in reality much more manly and less effeminate than those of *aujourd'hui*. As all fashions are very variable, so was this of short waists, as I experienced to my cost; for when, in 1807, we went out to Buenos Ayres, supposing our absence from home would be a long one, I took a complete and full outfit of everything, and among the rest three new jackets. These the nature of our service scarcely ever allowed me to wear half a dozen times, so that they were quite fresh when we returned to Woolwich, and to my horror, useless,—the mode being so completely changed that the jacket reached below the hips, and was made with something like the old-fashioned skirt. Long before this we had got rid of our flat lace—once thought so fine, now so mean—and our jackets were laced with the cord as at present. I think this change took place in 1806. But I have altogether omitted the 1st Horse Artillery jacket, or at least the first I recollect. I never remember seeing any other English troops wear such an one, but think it was the Chasseur jacket in the French Army.

1804.

1808.

1806.

Hooked at the collar, it sloped away toward the little skirt which terminated it behind, and had half facings. On the shoulders a sort of wing, made of interwoven rings; with leather breeches, long boots, and the helmet; this was rather a soldier-like service dress.

About 1805 we first began to wear pelisses, and poor shabby concerns they would be thought in the present day, although we then looked upon them as marvellously fine. They were trimmed with some brown fur, such as was then in common use for ladies' tippets, etc., perhaps sable—don't know; the braiding on the breast also was sparse and of very small cord. Altogether it was a shabby thing. Somewhere about 1808 the pelisse, only tolerated before, became a regular and authorized part of our uniform. The sable fur gave place to the grey astrachan, the braiding became richer with barrel buttons, and the whole affair more Hussarish.

Chaussure, etc.—Continuing my downward course to the nether man, we come next to his indescribables or inexpressibles—words which I must throw away for the present, since, although of not any very great importance, yet there are a few reminiscences connected with these articles not altogether uninteresting, which I must both express and describe. When I first got my commission, the Horse Artillery Officer clad his thighs in well-pipeclayed doe or buckskins; the Padnagge in well-whitened kerseymere, fastened at the knee with four small buttons and a buckle. These, for aught I can remember, constituted the one only pair of thigh-cases for each service. Morning parade, evening parade, wet weather or fine, breakfast, dinner, tea-party, ball or court—always white breeches. It was a sort of innovation when, after a time, the Foot Artillery assumed to themselves the skins, which eventually became also their uniform.

Dark blue pantaloons (cloth) began to creep in about 1802 (though they had always been worn by Officers on expeditions, etc.), and we were very proud of ourselves when at outquarters we could thus dress, as it looked so like service. So far is all I know of the Foot Artillery. (Blue pantaloons permitted by a General Order in 1803; see Kane.) In the Horse Artillery, besides our leather breeches, we wore the blue cloth pantaloons for common undress parades, and the same with gold lace for full dress, etc. The fronts of these were profusely decorated nearly halfway down the thigh, in the same style as worn by drum-majors of *aujourd'hui* (1840).

For marching order, we had blue cloth overalls, having leather down the inside of the thighs, and about the whole of the leg, in the shape of Hessian boots. These articles were then what the name implied, really overalls, being worn over pantaloons and buttoning from top to bottom outside; the pockets were in front of the groin,

1806.

set slopingly. To keep the overall down, instead of straps, we used chains, about the size and made like curb-chains, which, when walking about, instead of being under the foot, were suspended across the back of the leg by one of the buttons near the knee, as in the annexed. These chains, being kept highly polished, really looked very well, at least, to eyes of those days.

The dandyism of the day consisted in having them very long, half a yard, *par exemple* (for undress parades and common wear).

For dress, foot parades, etc., we had white stocking-net fitting quite as tight as the blue mentioned below. One of the Buenos Ayres Hussars fell desperately in love with a pair I wore at a ball, and teased me the whole night to sell them to him.

About the same period, I think, that we exchanged our flat lace for cord, we also got rid of our breeches and long boots in exchange for leather pantaloons and Hessian or Hussar boots. These, as well as the blue stocking net, which came in about the same time, were worn as tight as possible. (And about the same period the overall became simply trousers or pantaloons, merely retaining the fly as an ornament.)

At a subsequent period pepper-and-salt coloured overalls were worn, and the shades or tints of grey were altered more than once; but when this took place I know not now, nor can I call to mind when the red stripe down the side was introduced—I think somewhere about 1810 or 1811. At the same time the black leather inside the thighs, and boot below, gave place to brown leather, and instead of finishing in a boot, there was only a band of 3 or 4 inches round the bottes to save the cloth from the stirrup. The present purply half-tint was introduced in 1815. I remember Frazer showing me some of it one day at Paris, as a new thing.

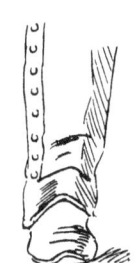

From breeches we slip down naturally to boots. The first time I saw the Hussar boot, it was worn by a very handsome, well-made man, and I thought it grand. Captain Foy had just arrived from Vienna, and I saw him at practice in the Warren, somewhere in 1798, for I was a Cadet. But the first boot I wore myself was the regimental one when I got my commission, up to the knee, with a stiff top, but not cut out behind, which

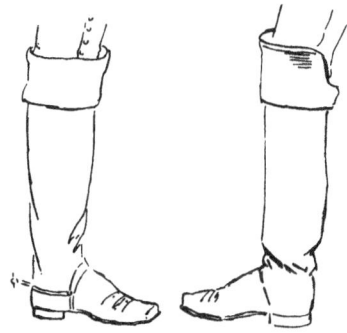

was then a piece of dandyism, and only became regimental afterwards. These boots were made large, and did not fit the leg; but when a Cadet, I remember the Officers wore a more flexible boot, fitting closely and showing the shape of the leg. This was kept up by a tongue attached to the kneeband of the breeches, and a buckle on the calf of the boot. The late father of the Regiment, General Sir John Smyth, when a Lieut.-Colonel, was an amazing beau, and flattered himself he had a good leg. Of course, his boots used to fit like gloves. The half-boots then 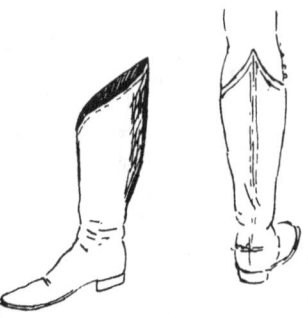 worn were the very reverse of what afterwards came in fashion, for instead of being higher in front, they were cut down and rose to a point behind. I remember Dr. Hutton sporting a pair. These were made with a single seam down the back, but subsequently it became quizzical not to have a double one, with a broad band between them. (The heels worn in 1804 by exquisites were very high and very small, tapering too; just such as women used to wear some forty or fifty years before, 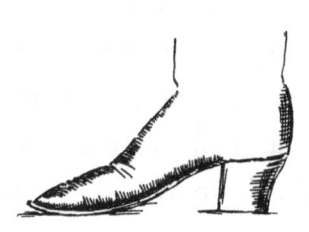 *par exemple.*) The Hussar boot is well known at the present day, rising in front, decorated with a silk tassel, and having a seam down each side. A sort of half-boot, rising in front like this, but having the double seam behind, became fashionable about the beginning of the century, and I shall not in a hurry forget the sensation caused at Plymouth Dock by Lieutenant Anderson (afterwards Colonel Morehead) making his appearance at the promenade in front of Government House one Sunday evening in a pair of these. "Oh, the puppy!" was heard on all sides. "If he has not silk tassels to his boots!" Only think! silk tassels on boots!

The greatest of all comforts and improvements, in my opinion, was when (after the general adoption of the trousers in imitation of overalls) we ceased casing our poor legs in leather, and substituted the short or ankle boot for the high Hussar.

Spurs, as a matter of course, follow boots, and there is little to be said on the subject. Like all other articles of dress, they went through a great variety of vagaries in the course of forty years. The first I remember worn by my father and by General or Field Officers was of silver, with a short bent neck, flat short branches, the deficiency in length made up by small chains, of silver also; this was the Field-

Officer's spur *par excellence*. The Horse Artillery (and I believe the Cavalry) used to wear a plated spur (the men's steel), with a long straight neck. It was not until 1805 or 1806 that we first began to wear spurs screwed on the heel of the boot. The form I do not remember, but think they had crooked necks. In 1807, I took out several pairs of new spurs in the most exquisite style of the day. These were very small, beautifully made and finished, of blue steel, and with straight, cocked-up necks. At Monte Video nothing could exceed the admiration of the Gauchos at sight of these elegant little spurs;—a striking contrast there was, to be sure, between them and their own huge misshapen silver ones. This is all that can be said about spurs,  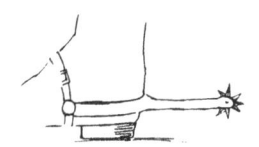  as far as I can recollect; but before dismissing the boot and its appendages I must say a word about the iron heels, which, like many other parts of our military costume, have been borrowed from the Germans. In 1802, the Hompesch Chasseurs à Cheval were quartered at Cork, and long shall I remember the impression produced whenever I met a party of these (dismounted) marching through the streets, the heavy tread of so many iron heels on the pavement, accompanied by regular clang of their steel scabbards and jingling of their carbine slings, the solemn unvarying features of their bronzed and mustachioed faces. To me there was something exquisitely picturesque and imposing in all this. We did not begin to wear iron heels for a year or two after this, my first recollection of them being in 1804.

And now, having taken the man from top to toe, or heel rather, we may advert to some minor articles of the toilette, and the adventitious circumstances connected with the decoration of the person, and so on.

Stocks, etc.—In the beginning of my career, the neck was enveloped in a black velvet stock, into which a padded stuffing was introduced to keep it up; or it was worn over a sufficient accumulation of white muslin, of which one-eighth of an inch in breadth was to border the upper edge of the stock as a finish. In plain clothes, white muslin cravats were then invariably worn, and none but masters or mates of merchantmen and such-like craft ever dreamed of wearing black. Captain (now Colonel) Birch of the Engineers was an exception, and it is curious to recall in the present day, when all wear black, the vulgarity imparted to his appearance by this departure from the established mode. At one period it was fashionable to wear cravats of immense size, or rather an immense number, one put on over the other, so as to form a mass of considerable thickness, in which the chin was buried almost up to the under lip. Whilst I wore this accumulation of cotton I was always subject to violent sore throat and stiff neck; in 1820 I left off every species of wrap that the usages of society would permit, and now for twenty years I have neither known one nor the other of these maladies. The eighth of inch white shown above the stock was intended for the men, and in their kits were included six false collars. These were narrow strips of linen, which were doubled over the leather stock and confined there by a hook at each end. The exact period when the shirt-collar began to be substituted in the shape of "dog's ears," I cannot precisely say, but think it must have been about 1810. In the Horse Artillery these became almost regulation, but I took it into my head that all black was more soldier-like, consequently would not wear them. One day when our two splendid troops were drawn up on Rushmere Heath, by Ipswich, ranks open, and every moment expecting the arrival of His Royal Highness George Prince Regent, by whom we were to be reviewed, Sir Augustus Frazer (then only Captain), who was one of the most precise little men in the world, happening to turn his head toward the lines to see that all was right, perceived me in front of G troop, all black, no dog's ears! Hastening to me, he begged that I would make myself like the rest by pulling up my collar, as the Royal Family were noted for their quick perceptions in all matters of military uniform. I told him my collar was too low. Dilemma! Frazer was not to be refused, and it ended by his tearing off the blank leaf of a letter he luckily had in his sabretasche, with which we fitted up a pair of dog's ears which answered perfectly to receive and march past His Royal Highness, and were thrown away as soon as we began to manœuvre.

Sashes.—I remember, when a boy, the old ones had a large boss or rose, whence the fringes depended; this was worn in front of left side, and was tied behind, under the coat with ribands. [The Hussar knotted sashes now worn by the Horse Artillery have been adopted since 1815. Up to that period they wore the net, with cords, such as we now see worn by Light Infantry and others.] I likewise remember only the rose and dependent fringe, which was attached by a broad flat hook of steel, stuck in the waistband. When I got my commission, we wore very large sashes of silk net that went several times round the body, and were admired in proportion. The idea was that, in case of being wounded, an Officer's sash ought to form a hammock to carry him in, by putting a pole through the two holes left next the knots, and then tying the stretched netting over his breast with ends of fringe cut off for the purpose.

Swords.—Nothing could be more useless or more ridiculous than the old Infantry regulation; it was good neither for cut nor thrust, and was a perfect incumbrance. In the Foot Artillery, when away from headquarters, we generally wore dirks instead of it. Generals, and our Field Officers, seemed to wear what they pleased, and after the Egyptian expedition the Mamaluke sabre was quite the rage. In the Horse Artillery, besides the large regulation sabre, we had a small undress one; but in the form of this we were not particular, every one adopting that most pleasing to his fancy, and this was usually so crooked as to be useless as anything but a reap-hook. The regulation itself, though an excellent sword for cutting, 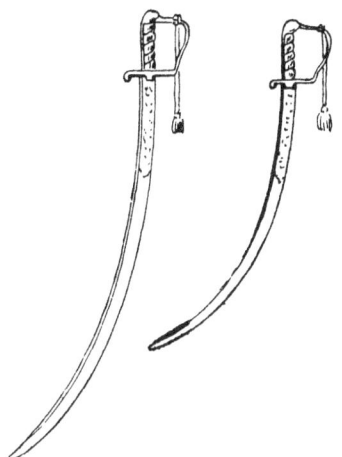 was bad for using the point, which was not so much insisted on in the drills then as now, since we have experienced the efficacy of the long French straight pusher. Dandyism with the sword was to wear it trailing along the ground, and some Cavalry beaux used to have a little treek or wheel in the end of the scabbard. It was common, nay, almost general, to have the points of the scabbards worn out by this trailing.

Fatigue Dress of Foot Artillery.—Perhaps in all the European armies there was not such another unmilitary costume as this, unless it were the smock frock worn by the French Infantry *en campagne*. This dress consisted of a long-backed coat of canvas or coarse duck, with skirts reaching below the calf of the leg, and huge copper buttons, a waistcoat and pair of loose trousers of the same, the bottom of these terminating in a kind of fringe. On the head the hideous leather cap mentioned (*ante*, p. 59), and on the feet strong shoes with bright brass clasps. When doing any heavy work, the men were obliged to twist up their skirts and tie them round the waist. The young second lieutenants, who were obliged to attend the laboratory, and to work themselves (not so now!) had each a dress of this sort to put on when he got there. These were kept in a lobby by the porter's lodge, and every man's name was painted in large letters on the back, not so much that he might readily find his own, but that the Captain, Adjutant, or other superintending officer might readily discriminate each as he sat at work, with his face to the wall and back to the centre of the workshop.

Cadets.—Under the article Hair, etc., I have mentioned these young gentlemen slightly; it would be a pity to pass over one of their tricks connected with the same. Whenever a new cadet joined, he was visited that very evening by a smart young journeyman barber, who politely informed him that it was the Captain's orders his (the cadet's) head should be put in order, that he might appear properly dressed at the next morning's parade. The youngster, all submission, sat himself down, the loquacious barber, whilst clipping away the honours of his head in a most unmerciful manner, all the while expatiating on the beauty of the locks thus barbarously scattered on the floor. The top, almost bare, was then rubbed back with a vigour that brought tears plentifully from the poor boy's eyes, and finally plastered thick with pomatum, to make it, as he was told, retain its form. Then came the queueing, an operation not less cruel nor more tenderly performed, the hair behind being gathered so close to the head, and bound together so tight, as to leave the unfortunate in an agony, and a certainty of not sleeping that night. This operation finished, the barber, after admiring the admirable transformation, and congratulating the youngster on the great facility with which his hair assumed a proper turn, suddenly assumed a graver tone and aspect, and, drawing himself up with outstretched palm, "Half a crown, if you please, sir." The coin once in his grasp, it sometimes happened that a coarse burst of laughter betrayed to the poor dupe the character of his visitor ere he was out of the room, though it was generally not until on the day following, when the true barber made his appearance, that he became aware of it, as also that the stuff with which his skull had been smeared, instead of pomatum, was an abominable mixture of soot, ashes, grease, and any filth that could be collected.

Organization, Parades, Drills, etc.—Connected with these subjects, the earliest peculiarity that I remember is, that when in Guernsey—in the years 1789 and 1790, the 8th and 12th Regiments used, in marching, always to have the band in the centre of the column. By this means, the sound arriving simultaneously at the first and last divisions, the step would be better preserved than in the present mode, since, in a long column with the band marching at its head, I have frequently observed the thump of the long drum marking the time for the left foot of the leading division coincide with the right foot of the rear, so that this last could only preserve the step by disregarding the drum.

Artillery Drills.—These, when I got my first commission, in 1799, went not beyond the serving of a gun and a few other things of a similar nature (manœuvring with drag-ropes, manning a gyn, etc.) We had no system of field exercises for a battery;

even in the Horse Artillery every commanding officer drew up something of his own. In telling off numbers to guns, we differed entirely from the mode at present in use. For garrison guns, they went from 1 upwards—1 sponges, 2 loads, etc.—For field guns, when there were drag-ropes they also began at 1, but then the first six were drag-rope men, and those serving the gun began at 7, which was the case when there were no drag-ropes; so that with a field gun it always ran thus: 7 sponges, 8 loads, 9 serves the vent, 10 fires, 11 commands (non-commissioned officer), 12 holds the cartouch, 13 brings up ammunition, etc. The first brigades (now called batteries) were formed by Major Spearman in 1800, and drilled by him at a set of manœuvres of his own drawing up. They consisted of medium 12-prs., I think six each (there were two brigades), drawn by six horses each, two and two, the drivers (then a new corps) mounted as postillions—quite a novelty. These two brigades were destined for Swinley camp. (None of the gunners were mounted, but marched beside the carriages.) At the same time Lieutenant (now Colonel) Wallace was drilling another brigade of light 6-prs. for the same destination, but to be attached as battalion guns to the Guards. The equipment of these was entirely different from Spearman's brigades. The guns were drawn by three horses each, with common cart harness and chain traces. These were conducted by contract drivers, dressed in canvas frocks, like our gunners' undress, with blue fall-down collars. One walked by the leader, the other by the wheelers, and both carried long waggon whips.

The latter end of the same year or spring of 1801, I was at Plymouth Dock when we were reviewed in the brickfield by General Grenville, a great soldier in those days. The style of this review was as follows: Our two (or trice) companies were formed in line to receive the General, whilst in our rear was drawn up our light 6-prs. (forget how many) in line also. After marching past and going through a few Infantry manœuvres, we broke into column from the original alignment, faced to right, filed through the intervals between the guns, piled arms in the rear, formed line of march at the guns, to which the men were already told off, and then commenced a series of Artillery movements and firing, all which we thought very grand, and I remember running myself into a most profuse perspiration in my zeal. General Grenville was highly pleased, paid compliments to General Stevens, who commanded (mark, a battery or a couple of companies commanded by a Major-General), and all the people said it was the most beautiful sight they had seen for a long while! In the following year, at Clonmel, we had civil artificers attached to our brigades, which was not unusual certainly, if not the general practice at that time. I mention this circumstance principally on account of a very ludicrous incident arising from it. The late Sir William Meadowes, then Commander of the Forces in Ireland, in the course of his progress on assuming the command, passed through and reviewed the garrison of Clonmel (28th Light Dragoons, Lancashire Fencibles, and our batteries, 12 and 6 prs.). Major Miller, who commanded us, was a very zealous excellent officer, but a most passionate though good man. Having formed his brigade in line, he drew up the artificers in continuation of it by themselves, with orders that when we marched past they should await us on the original ground. Amongst these characters was a wheeler, Burton, rather a large man, carrying a decent corporation, and that day dressed in his best coat, a long-backed, long-skirted garment of a lively plum-colour, with large white buttons. Mr. B. was a cross-grained, grumbling, chattering politician, wrong-side, of course, and loved of all things to thwart those in authority over him. On this occasion the fellow took it into his head that he was insulted in being left behind, when all the rest were exhibiting before the great man, and poor Major Miller's horror and rage may be better imagined than described, when, several paces in rear of the last division, he beheld Wheeler Burton, the long skirts of his long-backed, plum-coloured coat flapping against his calves, as he gravely strode along, chin in the air, the right hand, with its palm turned up, extended right out before him, with the emblem of his trade, his claw hammer, held erect between two fingers, and his eyes fixed with imperturbable insolence of gaze on the Commander of the Forces, who in his turn looked on with unmoved gravity, evidently taking Wheeler Burton for a legitimate part of the exhibition, whilst the Major was foaming with rage, every one else bursting with laughter.

Middlesex Militia.—I think it was in 1801 that Lieut.-General Simcoe reviewed this regiment, then quartered at Plymouth (in Mill Prison barracks), and commanded by a Colonel Bayley, a relation of Lord Uxbridge. This review was unique, for the first attempt at firing (a volley) betrayed the secret that, although they had come to the field provided with ammunition, they had forgotten to remove the wooden snappers and replace them by flints. The astonishment of all present may be imagined.

Horse Artillery.—I think it may not be amiss here to mention a few recollections which have occurred to me respecting this branch of the Artillery Service, which was first formed by the Duke of Richmond, then Master-General of the Ordnance, to whom it became a perfect hobby. It began by one troop, or what we should now call a battery, and this one, being completed, was immediately ordered to Goodwood, His Grace's residence, near Chichester, where the men and horses were easily lodged in the capacious stables and

GEORGE III.

rooms over them, with the guns parked in front of the house, His Grace having the new plaything immediately under his own eye. Whether the Duke only copied the idea of rapidly moving Artillery from the French, I know not, but the following, related to me by the late Sir Edward Howorth, himself a party in the transaction, who was one of the Duke's A.D.C.'s, may have something to do with it. Some French prisoners on board a ship lying off Southampton mutinied, and caused such an alarm in the place, where they had no artillery, that an express was sent in hot haste to Winchester for guns. Two 6-prs. were immediately equipped for the road, each to be drawn by four post-horses, driven by their respective postillions. The gunners were packed in post-chaises, and away they galloped, arriving in Southampton in time to overawe the Frenchmen and put an end to the tumult. This in some measure may have had its influence with His Grace in forming the first Troop Horse Artillery; be that as it may, he took great delight in its equipment, and, not being a practical soldier himself, had some whimsical ideas on the subject. The Officers were to have no baggage except such as was fixed by regulation, and for this purpose all the articles were furnished by the Board of Ordnance, and of one uniform pattern, viz. a small camp bed with curtains complete, and bedside carpet, all packed in boxes of uniform size; a small round octagonal hair trunk; a small camp table and two large camp stools; the bedding, of course, folded up to put in a painted canvas case. All the above-named articles, constituting the sole baggage of each troop Officer, were to be carried in the curricle cart. This vehicle consisted of a body with a roof like that of a house, with folding doors opening to the rear, mounted on a pair of wheels the same height as those of the gun, and two horses with a mounted driver. The packing required attention and some skill, for the load was so exactly calculated, and the boxes fitted so nicely, that when the load was finished you could hardly pass a straw between them. In after time the curricle cart still existed, but then it was exclusively devoted to the Officer Commanding.

The forge cart and its limber were fitted up in such a manner that, in case of necessity, the farrier could go at his work as they moved on. Then, to complete the whole, there was a covered waggon fitted up for the women, with tubs fixed in such a manner that all the operations of washing could go on without halting. This was the climax of absurdity; but although the Duke rode, as we see, his hobby-horse rather roughly, yet in all other respects he was a man of ability, both as a politician and as a Master-General; he was, moreover, extremely zealous in bringing both Engineers and Artillery to a state of perfection before unknown, except in the fooleries already mentioned. A troop of Horse Artillery, as organized by His Grace, was the most complete thing in the Army, and very few changes have taken place up to the peace of 1815. Except two gunners seated on each limber, the remainder were mounted, and were equipped as Light Dragoons of that day. In dress, however, they were somewhat different. The gunner wore on his head a helmet similar to that worn by all the Light Cavalry, but, instead of the black turban, theirs were red; again, instead of the road jacket worn by the Light Dragoons, the Horse Artilleryman wore one with short skirt somewhat resembling that of a Light Infantryman.

PLATE XIV.

AN OFFICER OF THE ROYAL ARTILLERY.

1820.

DESCRIPTION OF PLATE.

THE most remarkable feature to note in this plate is the change in the head-gear since Waterloo.

After having fought so long on the continent, and particularly against the French, the British Army had become greatly influenced by French fashions. The chako is distinctly of French origin, and the plate on it displays the old Board of Ordnance Arms. The Hessian boots with tassels were in vogue at this date.

AUTHORITIES.—Sketch entitled "The Garrison Staff, Woolwich." 1820.
Coloured print, "The Rotunda, Woolwich." 1820.

GEORGE IV.

1820—1830.

EORGE IV., as Regent and Sovereign, held the sceptre of Great Britain for twenty years, and during this period military fashions underwent considerable change.

Between the dates dealt with in this chapter (1820-1830), the peculiar taste of George IV. was shown in the extreme tightness of the uniform of Officers and men. The King is credited with saying that "in a military dress a wrinkle was unpardonable, but a seam was admissible;" and he carried his ideas to such an extent as to make his soldiers look ridiculous, and, worse than that, to seriously hamper them in the effective use of their weapons.

A story told of him in Luard's "History of the Dress of the British Soldier" illustrates his extraordinary penchant for tight clothes. "When the Lancer dress for the Officers was being selected, an Officer of rank commanding one of the Lancer regiments was ordered to attend George IV. (then Regent), to fit the new jacket on him; the tailor with a pair of scissors was ordered to cut smooth every wrinkle and fine draw the seams." These seams are said to have given rise to the piping in the Lancers' uniform of the present day.

1823. *August* 5.—R.H.A. leather pantaloons and Hessian boots were abolished; blue-grey overalls and Wellington boots substituted. (Kane's List.)

1824.—The short coat, white cloth pantaloons, and long boots of Officers were abolished. A long single-breasted coatee without any lace on the breast, blue-grey trousers with red stripes, and short boots substituted. The lace on the chako was discontinued, and replaced by black silk ferret. A new pattern plate for the shoulder

PLATE XV.

AN OFFICER OF THE ROYAL HORSE ARTILLERY.

1823.

Description of Plate.

Boots and breeches had been done away with since Plate XI.; Wellington boots and blue-grey overalls were now the fashion. The jacket was similar to that of the Waterloo period, as was also the helmet.

Shortly after this date the Horse Artillery helmet, which had been worn continuously since the formation of this branch of the service, was abolished, and a chako substituted instead of it. A cross-belt and sabretasche were also worn at this period.

AUTHORITIES.—Coloured print, Officer R.H.A. Heath, del. Published by Watson. 1820.

GEORGE IV.

belt, often called the breast-plate, was introduced, and in the summer season white drill trousers were ordered to be worn, which continued to 1841. A new pattern chako, with mohair plume for sergeants, and a woollen tuft for rank and file, introduced. Blue-grey trousers, with Wellington boots, ordered to be worn instead of white breeches and black gaiters. (Kane's List.)

1827. *September.*—A new pattern forage-cap for corporals, bombardiers, and privates. It was made of strong milled blue worsted, 12 inches across the crown, with a flat white button on the top, bound with black velvet. A white band 2 inches broad, chevrons in front. A black leather chin-strap.

December 22.—R.H.A. helmets were abolished; chako with tassels substituted.

Battalions.—Officers to wear embroidery (oak leaf with acorns) instead of lace on the coat; Captains and Lieutenants to wear an epaulette on the left shoulder, a strap on the right. For evening dress, Officers to wear blue cloth trousers, with gold lace stripes, $1\frac{3}{4}$ inch wide, down the outer seam. (Kane's List.)

1828. *July* 5.—Quarter-masters to wear a coat in all respects similar to other Officers, but without epaulettes and straps; cocked hat with regulation lace loop and bullion tassels and regulation feather; no sash. All other articles of dress the same as for other Officers. Waist-belt, black leather, worn on all occasions under the coat.

July 17.—Length of Officer's feather in the N.P. chako reduced to 10 inches. Feathers instead of tufts issued to non-commissioned officers and men. The dress taken into wear this year may be briefly described as follows:—

Coat.—Dark blue, double-breasted, with red collar and cuffs, and red turnbacks to the skirts. Officers' coats embroidered with gold oak leaf and acorn; sergeants', gold lace; rank and file, yellow worsted.

Epaulettes.—Officers, gold, with gilt crescent, and a silver embroidered grenade on the strap. Field Officers wore two, with device according to rank, bullion frequently loose. Company Officers, one on the right shoulder, and the strap without fringe on the left. Staff-sergeants, gold lace shoulder-strap, with fringe. Sergeants, red cloth shoulder-strap, with gold edging and fringe. Rank and file, red straps, with worsted lace and fringe.

Trousers.—Blue-grey, with red stripe 2 inches broad.

Boots.—Officers, Wellington; non-commissioned officers and men, ankle.

Chako.—Black, $6\frac{1}{2}$ inches high, with lacquered crown, $11\frac{1}{2}$ inches wide, with a half-inch rim; glazed straps sewn from top to bottom, a glazed strap 1 inch wide round the bottom, with a buckle behind. The cap plate was star-shaped, with device of three

PLATE XVI.

AN OFFICER OF THE ROYAL HORSE ARTILLERY.

1828.

DESCRIPTION OF PLATE.

HERE is seen the Horse Artillery chako with its enormous waving plume, cap-lines, and flounders (as the tassels were termed).

The overalls were worn very loose, and pleated in round the waist.

The sword-belt was worn low down on the hips.

Barrelled sashes were the fashion at this date.

AUTHORITIES.—Coloured print, Officer R.H.A. Hull, del. 1828.
    2 Coloured prints, Officers R.H.A., *Gentleman's Magazine of Fashion.* Heath, del. 1828.
    Coloured print, Officer R.H.A. Heath, del. Circa 1829.
    Print, "Artillerie Anglaise." Moltzheim, del. Circa 1830.
    2 Coloured prints, R.H.A. Heath, del. Circa 1831.
    2 Coloured prints, R.H.A. Martin, del. 1831.
    Painting, Officer R.H.A. Drusheme, del. 1833.

guns in silver. Officers and staff-sergeants wore a gold cap cord and tassels; other non-commissioned officers and privates, a worsted cord. (Kane's List.)

1830. *April* 22.—White linen trousers to be worn at home, from 1st May to 14th October. Cloth trousers the rest of the year.

May 28.—Quarter-masters to wear epaulettes similar to Subalterns.

September 23.—The cypher W.R. to be substituted for G.R.

November 16.—Officers' dress coat changed. Embroidery discontinued, and lace substituted. The epaulettes to be the same as ordered by the regulations of the Army. Captains and Subalterns to wear one on each shoulder. (Kane's List.)

PLATE XVII.

AN OFFICER AND GUNNER, ROYAL ARTILLERY.

1828.

DESCRIPTION OF PLATE.

THE grotesque appearance of the uniform at this time would be hard to beat.

Notice the wide-topped chako, with its enormous plume.

The trousers were worn very loose, and the coatees tight and high waisted.

AUTHORITIES.—2 Coloured prints, Officer and Gunner R.A. Hull, del. 1828.
 2 Coloured prints, Officer R.A., from *Gentleman's Magazine of Fashion*. Heath, del. 1828.
 Coloured print, title "Woolwich." Lami, del. 1829.
 Coloured print, Officer R.A. Heath, del. Circa 1829.
 Print, "Artillerie Anglaise." Moltzheim, del. Circa 1830.
 Coloured print, Royal Artillery. Heath, del. 1831.
 Coloured print, Royal Artillery. Martin, del. 1831.
 Water-colour sketch, "Gun Team R.A." 1835.

WILLIAM IV.

1830—1837.

WILLIAM IV., having followed the profession of a sailor, did not at first take much interest in the minor details of his army, and consequently there were very few alterations in dress when he came to the throne. Later on, however, towards the close of his reign, he evinced a great interest in military matters, and he instituted several radical changes in the uniform.

He considered that, scarlet being the national colour, the whole Army, with the exception of the Artillery and Rifles, should be clothed in it, and this change was therefore carried out. All light cavalry, with the exception of Hussars, were clothed, like the Infantry of the line, in scarlet. The Navy, whose facings for years had been white, were also ordered to wear facings of this colour.

1831.—General description of the dress to be taken into wear:—

Coat.—Blue, double-breasted, with two rows of buttons, nine in each row—device, crown and three guns—Prussian collar, scarlet fronts, with gold lace loop, $1\frac{1}{2}$ inch broad, rear part blue.

Cuffs.—Scarlet, $2\frac{1}{2}$ inches deep, blue sash flap on sleeve 5 inches long and $2\frac{1}{4}$ inches wide, with three loops of gold lace, $\frac{3}{4}$ inch broad, and three small buttons. Flaps of skirts, 7 inches long and 3 inches broad, with three loops and three

GUNNER R.H.A. (MARCHING ORDER), 1831.

large buttons, two large buttons on the waist, scarlet kerseymere turn-back skirt lining and edging. Skirt ornament, a crown over three guns, between sprigs of laurel, embroidered in gold. N.C.O.'s and men, same pattern as Officers, except the skirt ornaments, which were replaced by a small regimental button. Staff-sergeants and sergeants had gold lace, rank and file worsted.

Epaulettes. — Two for all ranks, all "box," *i.e.* with a rigid support to the bullion, which varied in depth and size: Colonel and Lieut.-Colonel, 3½ inches; Major, 3 in.; Captains and Subalterns, 2½ in. The other distinctions of rank were: Colonels, a crown and star upon the strap above the King's cypher; Lieut.-Colonels, a crown; Majors, a star of the bath, all surmounted with a silver grenade; Captains and Subalterns, a silver grenade only; staff-sergeants, gold bullion; sergeants, a red strap with gold lace and fringe; rank and file straps, worsted lace and fringe.

Trousers and Boots.—Same as in 1828.

Chako.—Same as in 1828. Feather reduced to 8 inches.

March 15. — Cap lines abolished. Leather stocks, heretofore issued to N.C.O.'s and men, to be provided at their own expense.

December 29.—R.H.A. jackets of the drivers assimilated to the gunners. Steel spurs of Officers abolished, brass spurs substituted. (Kane's List.)

1832. *January* 23.—Officers of Marching Battalions to appear at *levées* and drawing-rooms in the same dress as on parade. The white belt to be worn over the coat. The gold-laced trousers to be worn in evening dress as heretofore.

OFFICER R.H.A. IN UNDRESS UNIFORM (PELISSE), 1831.

OFFICER R.A. (FOOT) IN UNDRESS UNIFORM, 1831.

May 30. — The shoulder-belt, with slings, to be no longer worn by Field Officers; a buffalo leather waist-belt substituted. Field Officers to be distinguished by brass scabbards instead of steel ones.

September 14.—A new pattern belt-plate (breast-plate) introduced.

October 31.—A new cap-plate for Officers: gilt, with Royal Arms and supporters

WILLIAM IV.   83

a cannon below with "Ubique" over it, and the motto "Quo fas et gloria ducunt" below. This was taken into wear by Officers in 1833, by other ranks in 1834.

December 22.—A *shell jacket* approved for Officers at the following stations: Ceylon, West Indies, Cape of Good Hope, Mauritius, Mediterranean. Dark blue cloth, plain scarlet collar and cuffs, cuffs pointed on upper part of sleeve, gilt studs, hooks and eyes from bottom of collar down the front, gold four-platted cord shoulder-strap with two loops at the bottom, breast lining black silk. (Kane's List.)

GENERAL ORDER.

Deputy-Adjutant General's Office, Woolwich, 1st June, 1833.

THE King having been pleased to approve of the dress and appointments of General, Staff, and Regimental Officers and men of the Royal Artillery, the Master-General has ordered descriptions and Regulations to be drawn up and promulgated for the information and guidance of all Officers.

The Regulations have been printed, and copies will be distributed to Colonels and Field-Officers, to the several Battalion and Corp Offices, to all stations at home and abroad, and one copy to each troop and company throughout the regiment, which must be produced with the other books shown at inspections.

In communicating these Orders and Regulations, the Master-General calls on all Officers in command of Artillery, wherever stationed, to be particularly vigilant that the strictest attention be paid to every item, and that no alteration whatever be permitted. And he holds every Officer in command strictly responsible to enforce implicit obedience to these Orders from all Officers under their command; the smallest deviation from which will incur the Master-General's most serious displeasure.

A. DICKSON, Col.
D. A. Gen.

His Majesty having been pleased to grant the following mottoes for the Royal Artillery, viz. "UBIQUE" and "QUO FAS ET GLORIA DUCUNT," the word "Ubique" is to be substituted in lieu of all other terms of distinction hitherto borne on any part of the dress or appointments throughout the whole regiment, except in cases wherein the Royal Arms are borne in full, when the latter motto will be also inserted.

ROYAL HORSE ARTILLERY AND RIDING-HOUSE TROOP.

Dress.—The dress uniform is to be worn at *levées* and drawing-rooms, dress reviews, and birthdays.

Undress.—The undress is for general use, and to be worn on all occasions not otherwise specified.

Blue Frock-coat.—The blue frock coat may be worn as a common morning dress in quarters in summer, and the pelisse in winter; also on regimental courts-martial and courts of inquiry; regimental committees; orderly duty; inspections of barracks, hospitals, and necessaries; and on working-parties.

Undress Cap.—On these occasions an oiled-skin cap of the same shape and dimensions as the dress-cap, without plaits, ball, or excrescence for the socket of the feather, is to be worn, with a leather strap to fasten under the chin.

Sword.—Upon no occasion is an Officer to appear, whether in the jacket, pelisse, or frock-coat, without his sword.

Dress-cap.—The scales of the dress-cap are to be worn under the chin, upon all mounted duties, by the Officers, non-commissioned officers, and men. The leather strap, when off parade and upon dismounted duties.

Forage-cap.—The forage-cap may be worn in stables, and upon foraging or night-duties in the field; but it is not to be worn upon any parade or other duty; nor is it to be worn as a common morning dress in quarters.

Royal Horse Artillery and Riding-House Troop.

Dress.

Jacket.—Blue, with scarlet collar and cuffs; three rows of ball buttons at equal distances—the distance between the rows is $5\frac{1}{2}$ inches at top, and $1\frac{1}{2}$ at bottom—with royal cord loops, showing a quarter of an inch of the blue between each cord. Prussian collar, three inches deep, edged with two rows of Prussian braid; an edging of two rows of narrow gold braid round the jacket. An Austrian knot of Prussian braid, as on the collar, with figures on the sleeves, welt, and back.

Field Officers distinguished by a binding of flat lace round the collar and cuffs in addition.

Waistcoat.—Scarlet kerseymere, fastened with hooks and eyes, three rows of buttons, cords of narrow gold lace, $\frac{1}{2}$ inch between each cord, the intervals filled with narrow flat braiding, ornaments on the collar, and a narrow braiding entirely round.

Cap.—Black beaver, $6\frac{1}{2}$ inches deep, with lacquered sunk top $11\frac{1}{2}$ inches in diameter communicating with black leather stitched side-straps, with a band of the same, which is to encircle the bottom of the cap; black patent leather peak, with gold cords and tassels, the cords sufficiently long to pass under the right arm and fasten to the

WILLIAM IV.

third button of the left breast. Plate: the Royal Arms and supporters—a cannon below, with the mottoes "Ubique" above it, and "Quo fas et gloria ducunt" below, placed in front of the cap, and gilt scales on the sides; a leather strap to fasten under the chin upon dismounted duties, and when off parade.

Plume.—White drooping cock-tail feather.

Trousers.—Dark blue cloth, with a stripe of gold lace $1\frac{3}{4}$ inch wide down the outward seams.

Boots.—Ankle.

Spurs.—Yellow flat-sided, $2\frac{1}{2}$ inches long, including rowels.

Sword.—Regulation cavalry.

Scabbard.—Steel.

Sword-knot.—Gold acorn.

Sash.—Crimson, with five rows of gold barrels, and two gold tassels at the end of the cord.

Belt.—Blue Morocco leather, covered with gold lace 1 inch wide, and edged with blue velvet, without swivels, united with two lions' heads and an S hook.

Sabretasche.—Blue Morocco faced with blue cloth, with broad gold lace around it, within embroidered the Royal Arms and supporters—a cannon below, with the mottoes "Ubique" above it, and "Quo fas et gloria ducunt" below.

Stock.—Black silk.

Gloves.—White leather.

Undress.

Trousers.—Blue-grey cloth, with red stripes down each outer seam 2 inches wide.

Sword-knot.—Black leather.

Belt.—Black patent leather, $1\frac{1}{10}$ inch wide; plate gilt; device, the Royal Arms, encircled with a wreath of the rose, shamrock, and thistle, surmounted by a crown, and with the motto "Ubique" beneath; to be worn over the frock-coat.

Sabretasche.—Black patent leather, badge gilt; the King's Arms with supporters—motto "Ubique" beneath.

Pelisse.—Blue, with black mohair royal cord, and a narrow braid between the intervals; barrel buttons, and trimmed with black Astrachan lambs' fur, lined with scarlet plush.

Jacket, Waistcoat, Cap, with Oiled-skin Cover, Boots, Spurs, Sword, Scabbard, Cravat, Gloves.—The same as in Dress.

Valisse.—Blue cloth, with round ends, edged with gold cord, and R.H.A. at each end.

Forage-cap.—Blue cloth, with patent leather peak, band of gold lace $1\frac{7}{10}$ inch broad, of the same pattern as on the sabretasche, with a convex gold button on the crown.

Frock-coat.—Blue cloth, with Prussian collar, black mohair braiding $\frac{3}{4}$ inch wide; back and skirt ornaments of the same; Austrian knot on the sleeves.

Sash.—Plain crimson, barrelled.

Dismounted Dress Parades.

Trousers.—From 1st May to 14th October—white linen or duck.

Horse Furniture.

Review Order.

Saddle.—Hussar.

Shabracque.—Blue cloth, with gold lace, 2 inches wide round the edges; the ends of the flaps rounded off; without tassels.

Sheepskin.—Black, edged with scarlet cloth.

Bridle and Bit.—Brown leather, ornamented with rosettes of the same; gilt bosses of regimental pattern; head collar and reins.

Field Day Order.

Saddle.—Hussar.

Shabracque.—Plain blue cloth, the ends rounded off; without tassels.

Sheepskin.—As in Review Order.

Bridle and Bit.—As in Review Order.

Marching Order.

The same as in Field-day Order, with the addition of the valisse.

Cloak.—Blue cloth, with scarlet collar.

Gun Drill Order and Practice.

Saddle.—Hussar stript.

Non-Commissioned Officers and Men.

Gloves.—White leather.

WILLIAM IV.

Undress.

Forage-cap.—The staff-sergeants and sergeants wear the same as the Officers, but without a peak; the lace of regimental pattern; the chevrons of sergeants, gold lace in front above the band.

Corporals, bombardiers, gunners, drivers, artificers, and trumpeters, dark blue, strong-milled worsted, 12 inches across the crown, with a flat white button on the top, bound with black velvet; white tape band 2 inches wide, and black leather chin-strap. The chevrons of the rank in white in front above the band.

BATTALIONS.

The only distinction of dress and undress for Officers of the battalions of Artillery is, that dark-blue cloth trousers, with gold lace stripes, are to be worn in the winter, at court, and in the evening.

The Coatee.—Is to be worn upon all parades (unless the men are ordered to be in fatigue dress), at divine service, on guards and piquets, public field-days, general inspections, funeral parties, general, district, and garrison courts-martial and courts of inquiry, boards of Officers for pensioning soldiers, public and probationary examinations of gentlemen cadets.

The Sash.—Is to be worn upon all occasions with the coatee, and with the blue frock-coat when upon duty.

Belts.—Regimental Field-Officers and Adjutants are always to wear the white waist-belt, and Company Officers the shoulder-belt, with the coatee; with this exception, that at mess and in the evening the Company Officers are to wear the black waist-belt under the coatee, and the sash over it.

Brevet Field-Officers, in garrisons where they are allowed forage, and take the duty of Field-Officers of the day, are to wear brass scabbards and white waist-belts, as laid down for Regimental Field-Officers, unless the Officer commanding the troops dispenses with it.

GUNNER R.A. (UNDRESS), 1833.

The blue frock-coat is to be worn as a common morning dress in quarters, and upon the following duties: parades, drills, practice, and Artillery exercises, at which the men are ordered to be in fatigue dress; working parties, inspections of barracks, hospital and necessaries, orderly duty and upon the march, regimental courts-martial, courts of inquiry, and committees.

The black waist-belt is to be worn upon all occasions with the frock-coat, excepting by Adjutants, who are always to wear the *white* waist-belt; and when any Officer is engaged upon a duty of any description, the sash is to be worn.

Sword.—Upon no occasion is an Officer to appear, whether in the coatee or frock-coat, without his sword.

Covered Cap.—With the blue frock-coat an oiled-skin covered cap, of the same shape and dimensions as the dress-cap, without the plaits, ball, or excrescence for the socket of the feather, is to be worn, with a leather strap to fasten under the chin.

Dress-cap.—The scales of the dress-cap are to be worn under the chin, upon all mounted duties, by the Officers, non-commissioned officers, and men; the leather strap, when off parade and upon dismounted duties.

Forage-cap.—The forage-cap may be worn in stables, and upon foraging or night duties in the field; but it is not to be worn upon any parade or other duty; nor is it to be worn as a common morning dress in quarters.

Battalions.

Coatee.—Dark blue, double breasted, with 2 rows of buttons (crown and 3 guns, gilt), 9 in each row, at equal distances, the distance between the rows to be 3 inches at top, and $2\frac{1}{2}$ at bottom. Prussian collar, scarlet fronts $6\frac{1}{4}$ inches at bottom, and $7\frac{1}{2}$ at top, with gold lace loop; loop $1\frac{1}{2}$ inch broad, rear part blue. Cuff, scarlet, $2\frac{1}{2}$ inches deep; blue slash flap on sleeve, 5 inches long, and $2\frac{1}{4}$ inches wide, with 3 loops of gold lace, and 3 small buttons. Gold lace on slashes and flaps, $\frac{3}{4}$ inch broad. Flaps on skirts, 7 inches long, and 3 inches broad, with 3 loops and 3 large buttons; 2 large buttons on waist; scarlet kerseymere turnbacks; skirt lining and edging; skirt ornaments, crown over 3 guns between sprigs of laurel, embroidered in gold. Body-lining, scarlet shalloon.

Epaulettes.—Two for each Officer.

Field-Officers: box with plain gold lace strap, solid crescent, embroidered badge of King's cypher; bullion for Colonel and Lieutenant-Colonel is to be $3\frac{1}{2}$ inches deep; that of Major, 3 inches.

WILLIAM IV.

Captains: box with gold lace strap, with narrow silk red stripes, solid crescent; bullion smaller than that of a Major, and 2½ inches deep.

Subalterns: the same as Captains, except that the bullion is smaller.

Colonels are to have a crown and star upon the strap, above the King's cypher.

Lieutenant-Colonels a crown, and Majors a star of the Order of the Bath, all surmounted with a silver grenade.

Captains and Subalterns are to have only a silver grenade on the strap.

Cap.—Black beaver, 6½ inches deep, with lacquered sunk top 11½ inches in diameter, communicating by black leather stitched side-straps, with a band of the same, which is to encircle the bottom of the cap; black patent leather peak; plate, the Royal Arms and supporters—a cannon below, with the mottoes "Ubique" above it, and "Quo fas et gloria ducunt" below it, in front of the cap, and gilt scales on the sides; a black leather strap to fasten under the chin upon dismounted duties, and when off parade.

Feather.—White upright hackle, 8 inches long.

Trousers.—From 15th October to 30th April, blue-grey cloth with red stripes, 2 inches wide down each outer seam, fastened at bottom with a black strap.

From 1st May to the 14th October, white linen or duck, with black straps at bottom. For evening dress only, dark blue cloth with gold lace stripe, 1¾ inch wide, down the outward seam.

Boots.—Ankle.

Spurs.—For mounted Officers, yellow metal, flat-sided, with necks 2½ inches long, including rowels.

Sword.—Gilt half-basket hilt, as established for Infantry.

Scabbard.—Regimental Field-Officers, brass; other mounted Officers, steel. Company Officers not attached to field batteries, and all ranks at Court, black leather with gilt mountings.

Sword-knot.—Crimson and gold, with bullion tassel.

Belts and Plates.—Regimental Field-Officers: white buffalo leather waist-belt, $1\frac{7}{10}$ inch wide, with slings; plate, gilt; device, the Royal Arms, encircled with a wreath of the rose, shamrock, and thistle, surmounted by a crown, and with the motto "Ubique" beneath.

Adjutants: white buffalo leather waist-belt, 2 inches wide, with slings; plate, gilt; the same device as on the Field-Officers', above described.

Company Officers: white buffalo leather, 3 inches wide, worn diagonally over the shoulder, with slings; plate, gilt; device, similar to that on the waist-belts, with the addition of a field-piece below the "Ubique," and a second motto, "Quo fas et gloria ducunt," under the cannon.

A black patent leather waist-belt, 2 inches wide, with slings; plate, gilt, similar to that worn by Adjutants, described above, is to be worn with the frock-coat by all Officers, excepting Adjutants.

The slings for suspending the swords are to be of such length as not to suffer the sword to trail on the ground.

Sash.—Patent net crimson silk, with bullion fringe ends. The sash to go twice round the waist, and to be tied on the left hip (mounted Officers' on the right), the pendent part to be uniformly one foot in length from the tie.

Cravat or Stock.—Black silk.

Gloves.—White leather, or Berlin.

Shell-jacket.—Dark blue cloth, scarlet collar and cuffs without lace, cuffs pointed on upper part of sleeve, small vent at bottom, gilt studs, hooks and eyes from bottom of collar down the front; gold four-platted cord shoulder-straps, with two turns at bottom; breast lining, black silk. To be worn at the following stations, viz. Ceylon, Mauritius, Cape of Good Hope, Gibraltar, Mediterranean, West Indies, Canada, and Bermuda.

Frock-coat.—Blue cloth, single breasted, quite plain, with Prussian collar, 8 regimental buttons down the front, and 2 small ones for the cuff.

Forage-cap.—Blue cloth, with patent leather peak, band of gold lace $1\frac{7}{10}$ inch broad, with a convex gold button on the crown.

Cloak.—Blue cloth, walking length, lined with scarlet shalloon; gilt clasps at bottom of the collar.

Horse Appointments.

Saddle-cloth.—Scarlet, of 2 feet 10 inches in length, and each flap 1 foot 10 inches in depth, with one row of gold lace $\frac{3}{8}$ of an inch wide, and blue edging.

Bridle.—Of black leather, bent branch-bit with gilt bosses of regimental pattern.

Collar.—White.

Holsters.—Covered with black bear-skin, except in tropical climates, when they are to be covered with black leather.

WILLIAM IV.

Valisse.—Plain dark blue cloth, with round ends, 18 inches long, and 6 inches diameter of ends.

BATTALIONS.

Fatigue Dress for Non-commissioned Officers and Men.

Jacket.—Staff-sergeants: none.

Sergeants, corporals, bombardiers, gunners and drivers, and artificers: round dark blue cloth, without skirts; scarlet collar, without lace, single-breasted, a row of small regimental buttons (fourteen in number) down the front, and one button on each cuff; yellow worsted platted cord shoulder-straps, and lined with white serge. Chevrons, according to rank: sergeants, of gold lace; corporals, etc., yellow worsted lace; drummers and trumpeters, the same description, in scarlet, with blue collar.

Trousers.—Blue-grey cloth, with scarlet stripes, 2 inches wide down the outward seams, without pockets.

Fatigue-cap.—Staff-sergeants: dark blue cloth, with crown $12\frac{1}{2}$ inches diameter; a bee-hive gold ornament on top, depth $5\frac{1}{2}$ inches, gold lace band, 2 inches broad, of the same pattern as on the coatee; black leather peak, and black leather chin-strap.

Sergeants, the same, but without a peak; and in addition, 3 gold lace chevrons, in front above the band.

Corporals, bombardiers, gunners and drivers, artificers, and drummers and trumpeters: blue, strong milled worsted, 12 inches across the crown, with a flat white button on the top, bound with black velvet; white band, 2 inches broad, and black leather chin-strap; the chevrons of the rank in white, in front and above the band.

Staff-sergeants may wear an oiled-skin covered cap on undress occasions, when the officers wear them.

Gloves.—Staff-sergeants and sergeants, white leather; corporals, bombardiers, gunners and drivers, artificers, and drummers and trumpeters, white worsted.

1834. *May* 26.—Cross-belts abolished for R.H.A., and waist-belts substituted.

August 9.—Officers of Foot Artillery to wear, with the blue frock-coat, shoulder-straps of blue cloth, laced round, and solid crescent, fastened with a brass tongue and gold binder. Field Officers to have crown and star and a grenade upon shoulder-straps, as these are now worn upon the straps of their epaulettes. Captains and Lieutenants to wear a grenade upon the shoulder-strap, within the crescent. (Kane's List.)

VICTORIA.

1837—1897.

THE reign of Queen Victoria may be conveniently divided into two epochs, as regards the dress of the Army, viz. from 1837 to 1854, and from 1854 to the present time.

Prior to 1854, the military taste, or rather the taste of those in office, was still greatly influenced by the Georgian period. Large unwieldy head-dresses with enormous plumes, and high collars with stiff leather stocks, were worn. The jackets and coatees were very tight and short-waisted, with tight long sleeves. Loose trousers or overalls were also worn, and the dress was more ornate and less serviceable.

At the time of the Crimean War all this was changed, and the very opposite extreme was reached. Loose tunics with long skirts and very low collars, very wide full sleeves, a diminution in lace, and a certain slackness and appearance of ease, came into fashion. Latterly there has been an increasing tendency to make the dress of the Army more serviceable, and the number of different uniforms hitherto required by each Officer has been considerably diminished.

1837. Bearskin busbies for R.H.A., substituted for chakos.

January 28.—General Officers to wear, with blue frock-coats, a small aiguillette on the right shoulder, instead of the gold and crimson cord.

September 5.—N.P. forage-cap, of dark blue cloth, red piping round the edge of crown, and red band. Staff-sergeants and sergeants to wear a gold lace band above the red one, and peak. (Kane's List.)

1838. *March* 31.—*Officers' coatee:* gold lace abolished and embroidery substituted. A full red collar and N.P. button introduced. Skirts to be plain, with embroidered

PLATE XVIII.

AN OFFICER AND GUNNER, ROYAL ARTILLERY.

1840.

DESCRIPTION OF PLATE.

THE figures here depicted wore one of the ugliest and most unserviceable uniforms ever invented by man.

This was the last year in which white trousers were worn; they were abolished in 1841.

The uniform of both Officers and men underwent very slight change since 1828.

This was the uniform worn at the time of Queen Victoria's accession.

AUTHORITIES.—Coloured print, "Royal Artillery." Heath, del. 1840.
Coloured print, "Guard-mounting, R.A." Hayes, del. 1840.
Orders of Dress as quoted in text.

grenade at bottom. *Epaulette*: a gold bullion crescent substituted for the gilt plate, and three embroidered guns within the garter, with "Ubique" on the strap, instead of grenade. *Sword-knot*: tassel to be round instead of flat. *Cossack boot* substituted for laced boots, for non-commissioned officers and men.

April 11.—N.P. *frock-coat* for Officers, to be doubled breasted, with two rows of buttons, and red piping round outer edges. Shoulder-strap to be metal (scale pattern) with an ornament containing three guns enclosed in the garter, and "Ubique" within the crescent.

April 29.—Embroidered grenade, to be worn on the collar of Officers' shell jacket, similar to that on frock-coat.

May 18.—The white drill trousers to be made to button up the front, instead of with a flap (as heretofore). (Kane's List.)

1839. For R.H.A. plumes altered.

May 9.—N.P. cap and plume introduced.* Chako, black beaver, 6 inches deep in front and 7½ inches behind, with sunk crown 10 inches in diameter, and a black patent leather stitched strap round the edge, a band of same to encircle bottom of cap. Black patent leather peak, 2¾ inches wide. Plate, a crown and star below, on which is an unlimbered gun with "Ubique" underneath it. A black patent leather strap to fasten under the chin, with buckle on right side. Plume, hair upright, 8 inches long.

December 7.—Patent leather stock substituted for the leather (common) one, for non-commissioned officers and men. (Kane's List.)

1840. *May* 1.—Adjutants to wear sabretasche, with buff slings. (Kane's List.)

1840.—The dress of non-commissioned officers and men altered to meet alterations in Officers' dress (made in 1838), viz. the collar to be full red and laced round with yellow lace half-inch wide at top and bottom, with a small embroidered grenade on each side of the front part between the rows of lace. The flaps on the skirts taken off, and the latter made heavier. The slashes on cuffs laced round instead of across. N.P. button, having three guns and a crown over them, and a scroll with "Ubique" beneath on a sunken die.

October 5.—Officers, while attached to field batteries, to wear a shell jacket at all undress parades, instead of frock-coat. (Kane's List.)

Circa 1840.—Scarlet coatees and light blue trousers were worn at this period by drummers and trumpeters. The scarlet coatee was worn by them up to 1850, when a

---

* N.P. cap and chako taken into wear 1840.

THE DRUM-MAJOR OF THE ROYAL REGIMENT OF ARTILLERY.

Circa 1840.

DESCRIPTION OF FRONTISPIECE.

THE plate represents the Drum-Major of the Royal Artillery about the year 1840. This full-dress uniform was unique, it being almost the last date on which scarlet was worn by Drummers and Trumpeters; the Drum-Major was also much more ornately clothed at this date than at any other, before or after. The busby was enormous in proportion to the height of the figure.

FRONTISPIECE.—The Drum-Major of the Royal Regiment of Artillery. Circa 1840.

AUTHORITIES.—Coloured print of "The Drum-Major of the Royal Artillery." A. Comer, 1st D. Gds., del. Published by E. Jones (no date).
Water-colour drawing of Trumpeter R.A., 1840. W. Heath, del.
Coloured print, Royal Artillery, 1840. No. 2. W. Heath, del. Published by Ackermann.
MS. Notes descriptive of the uniform worn by the Drum-Major, Trumpeters, and Drummers of the R.A. By G. R. Hunter, Esq.

VICTORIA.

few in each battalion got blue, the remainder wearing scarlet. In 1851 the issue of blue was made general. Light blue trousers were discontinued in 1847, and dark blue ordered to be taken into wear.

At Woolwich only, about 1840, drummers and trumpeters were, unless attached to field batteries, always colloquially styled "drummers;" elsewhere, as the use of the drum became gradually discontinued, they were called "trumpeters."

Also it is worthy of note that at this period, although the scarlet coatee was generally worn, drummers and trumpeters always wore blue fatigue jackets when away from Woolwich; that is, they never provided themselves with scarlet coatees elsewhere. During the forties, a drummer fully equipped in heavy marching order wore full regimentals, with chako, and brass-hilted sword. On his back, knapsack, with great-coat rolled on top, and canteen behind. He carried a side-drum, deeper than those in use now, enveloped in a ticking cover, a brass fife-case, sometimes two. A trumpet similar to those now in use, and a bugle very much larger than the present ones.

Drummers and Trumpeters, circa 1840.

Kit carried in knapsack in heavy marching order:—

- 2 linen shirts.
- 1 flannel shirt.
- 1 towel.
- 2 pairs worsted stockings.
- 1 hold-all, containing knife, fork, spoon, razor and case, pocket-knife, hair-brush and comb, soap-bag, and shaving-brush.
- 1 Bible.
- 1 Prayer-book.
- 1 button stick and brush.
- 1 tin, brass ball.
- 1 sponge.
- 1 pair shoe-brushes.
- 1 tin blacking.
- 1 cloth-brush.
- 1 forage-cap.
- 1 fatigue jacket.
- 1 pair trousers.
- 1 pair Wellington boots.

AUTHORITY.—MS. Notes descriptive of the Uniform worn by Trumpeters and Drummers of the Royal Artillery. By G. R. Hunter, Esq.

1841. *March* 18.—White trousers not to be worn in Great Britain and Ireland and Channel Islands by non-commissioned officers and men.

PLATE XIX.

AN OFFICER OF THE ROYAL HORSE ARTILLERY.

1850.

Description of Plate.

This was the uniform worn by Officers of the Horse Artillery from about 1846 to the time of the Crimea. The chief difference between this plate and the last is the alteration in the head-gear from a chako to a bearskin busby, a jacket with five instead of three rows of buttons, and dark blue overalls instead of blue-grey.

The shabracque was also modernized.

Authorities.—Coloured print, Officer R.H.A. Giles, del. 1842.
Two Coloured prints, Officers R.H.A. Jones, del. 1843-1845.
Coloured print, R.H.A. Hayes, del. 1846.
Coloured print, Officer R.H.A. Martens, del. 1844.
Coloured prints, R.H.A. Campion, del. 1850.
Coloured print, R.H.A. Martens, del. 1853.
Coloured print, Officer R.H.A. Campion, 1854.
Coloured print, R.H.A. 1855.
R.H.A. jacket
   „   busby and plume } 1854. In R.A. Institution Museum.
   „   barrelled sash

VICTORIA.

March 22.—A lighter grenade and smaller plume to be worn by Officers in the chako. (Kane's List.)

1845.—Sergeants of the Marching Battalions discontinued carrying halberts (see 1754). (Kane's List.)

1846. *January* 14.—N.P. patent leather stock for non-commissioned officers and men.

April 22.—N.P. regimental cap for Officers, non-commissioned officers, and men, with brass curb.

May 31.—N.P. chako: felt cylinder, 7 inches high and 8 inches in diameter, having a rim 1 inch in depth, and stitched through within ⅛ inch of its edge. Front peak 2½ inches rear, 1¼ inch in depth. A leather strap, 1 inch broad, round the cap, close above the peaks and buckle behind. Plate of brass, device: the Royal Arms, with a gun below, having "Ubique" above and "Quo fas," etc., below it. Brass chain scales to be worn under chin. Plume, white horsehair, 6 inches long, attached to the cap by a brass fuze. (Kane's List.)

OFFICER R.A. (FOOT) IN UNDRESS UNIFORM, 1846.

1847. *January* 11.—Dark blue trousers to be taken into wear from April 1, and light blue discontinued from July 1. (Kane's List.)

1849. *April* 30.—Officers' sword-knot altered to gold cord, with acorn. Waist-belt, white patent buffalo leather with slings. Gilt plate, device: Royal Arms, circled by a wreath of rose, shamrock, and thistle, with "Ubique" underneath. (Kane's List.)

1850. *October* 21.—Master gunners to wear a forage-cap, similar to the staff-sergeants, instead of the plain round hat with cockade. (Kane's List.)

1851. *December* 17.—Sergeants, blue great-coats to be furnished with scarlet collar. (Kane's List.)

1853.—Sealskin substituted for bearskin busbies (for R.H.A.). (N.B.—Officers continued to wear the bearskin busby till 1855.)

DRIVER R.A., 1846.

PLATE XX.

A FIELD OFFICER AND GUNNER, ROYAL ARTILLERY.

1854.

Description of Plate.

It has already been stated that Queen Victoria's reign is divided into two epochs. This plate represents the uniform worn at the end of the first epoch.

For the last time are seen the chako, coatee with high collar, stock, and large epaulettes.

It will be noticed that waist-belts instead of cross-belts were worn, but otherwise the dress was similar to that of Plate XVIII.

Authorities.—Coloured print, Royal Artillery. Campion, del. 1850.
Coloured print, Royal Artillery. Martens. 1853.
Coloured print, Royal Artillery. 1855.
Coatee
Chako and plume
Shoulder-belt and breastplate } 1854. In R.A. Institution Museum.
Sword and sash

September 22.—Non-commissioned officers' and men's forage-cap altered as follows: depth of wall, 1¾ inch; width of band, 1¼ inch; diameter of crown to be in proportion to size of head. (Kane's List.)

1854.—R.H.A. Officers' pelisse abolished.

November 7.—N.P. chako with black oilskin case, and plume.

November 20.—The O.P. chako and plume to be continued to be worn until further orders. (Kane's List.)

1855.—Sable substituted for busby now worn by R.H.A. Cross-belts of gold lace, with pouch for Officers. Lace reduced on full-dress jacket.

R.H.A. frock-coat and red undress waistcoat abolished, and plain blue stable jacket adopted.

May 16.—Frock-coat, similar to that of R.H.A. Officers, approved for Officers of Battalions. In review order, Officers to wear gold-laced appointments, and laced trousers.

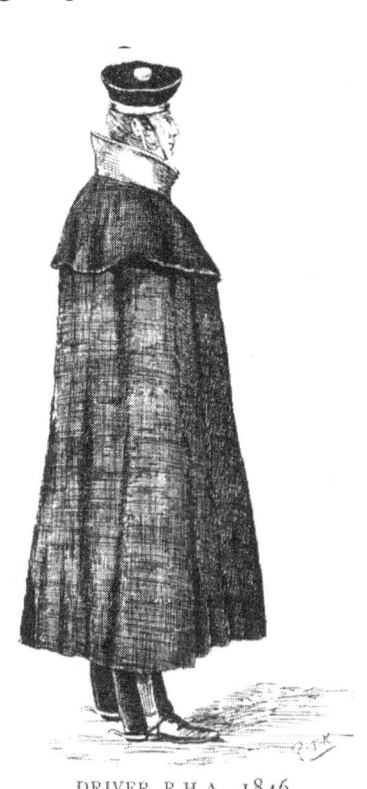

DRIVER R.H.A., 1846.

June 5.—Busby introduced in lieu of chako, and a tunic in lieu of coatee. (N.B.—Taken into wear April, 1856.) Epaulettes abolished. (Kane's List.)

1856. *January* 30.—Stable jacket, blue, single breasted, scarlet collar, gold lace, and distinguishing badges for ranks.

July 7.—Mounted Officers to wear swan-necked spurs.

November 25.—Peak removed from the forage-cap of sergeants. (Kane's List.)

1857.—R.H.A. The plume shortened from 12 to 8 inches. Swan-necked steel spurs for Officers and men, in lieu of brass spurs for Officers and straight steel spurs for men. Booted leather overalls introduced.

July 14.—Alterations in dress. *Colonel:* collar laced all round, with gold lace inside the gold cord; chevron of flat gold lace, 1½ inch wide, with three rows of small gold braid outside the chevron, two rows figured, the centre one plain, 11 inches deep; crown and star. *Lieut.-Colonel:* same as above, with crown only. *Brevet-Major:* star.

OFFICER R.H.A. IN UNDRESS UNIFORM (PELISSE), 1854.

Plate XXI.

A FIELD OFFICER AND TRUMPETER OF THE ROYAL HORSE ARTILLERY.

1855—1871.

Description of Plate.

This plate represents the dress worn at the early part of the second epoch of Queen Victoria's reign, and differs widely from the last.

Very loose sleeves, low collars, and booted overalls were all features of this period. In fact, the style of dress was much more like that of the present day.

Long hair and bushy side-whiskers were fashionable at this time.

Authorities.—Photographs in R.A. Institution. 2 vols.
Uniform of the period in existence.
Dress Regulations, Royal Artillery. 1855.
Dress Regulations, Royal Artillery. 1864.

VICTORIA.

Captain and *Lieutenant*: collar laced round top with gold lace and gold cord; sleeve ornament, Austrian knot of regulation gold cord, traced in and out with small gold braid, 8 inches deep, and figured. For Captain, 7 inches deep, and plain for Lieutenant. *Collar badges:* Captain, crown and star; Lieutenant, silver embroidery. *Field-Officers* to wear distinctive badges on collar, in gold, on frock-coat. *Stable jacket:* Blue, single breasted, scarlet collar, gold Russian braid all round the collar and jacket, terminating at each hip in a figure of 8; sleeves trimmed according to rank; holes and buttons down front 1¾ inch apart, 2 buttons at each wrist, lining white. *Beard* worn during Crimean War, and discontinued in autumn of 1856. *Moustache* then ordered to be continued.

September 25.—Serge trousers to be worn as a summer dress, same as worn by Infantry.

December 24.—Mounted non-commissioned officers and drivers to wear booted trousers. (Kane's List.)

1858. *February* 2.—Driver non-commissioned officers, farriers, and drivers furnished with valise, in lieu of knapsack. (Kane's List.)

OFFICER IN UNDRESS, 1856.

1859. *January* 28.—Colonels on the Staff, and Colonels commanding districts, to wear the regulation cocked hat instead of the busby.

March 24.—Busby sloped off behind, and lengthened towards the neck.

July 15.—Medical officer and veterinary surgeons to wear a black Morocco shoulder-belt and case.

September 28.—Worsted chevrons for great-coats of non-commissioned officers.

October 9.—Non-commissioned officers and men, figures on the shoulder-straps of tunic and jacket, denoting brigades. (Kane's List.)

1860. *April* 19.—Peak of Officers' forage-cap discontinued. (Kane's List.)

1861. *February* 26.—A pair of leggings issued to non-commissioned officers and gunners.

March 14.—N.P. forage-cap (to be made from the skirts of the tunic) introduced for rank and file, dark blue cloth, 3¼ inches high, size of crown and lower edge to be the same, yellow worsted band, 1¾ inch wide, yellow button in centre of crown, leather chin-strap, with black buckle. (Kane's List.)

PLATE XXII.

A FIELD OFFICER OF FIELD ARTILLERY AND A GUNNER OF GARRISON ARTILLERY.

1864.

Description of Plate.

With the exception of the difference between the Horse and Field Artillery, the style of dress is very similar to the last plate (No. XXI.). It is interesting to notice the old Artillery busby.

Contrasting the garrison gunner with the gunner in Plate XX., the difference in dress is most striking, the busby instead of the chako, and the tunic instead of the coatee.

Authorities.—Coloured print, "Officer R.A." Martens, del. 1855.
Coloured print, "Royal Artillery." Thomas, del. 1861.
Coloured print, "Royal Artillery." Sharpe, del. 1856.
Photographs in R.A. Institution. 2 vols.
Uniform of the period in existence.
Dress Regulations, Royal Artillery. 1855.
Dress Regulations, Royal Artillery. 1864.
Dress Regulations for the Army. 1874.
Plates in "Standing Orders of the Royal Regiment of Artillery." 1876.

VICTORIA.

1862. *March* 15.—Clothing of Officers serving in North America to be:—*Frock-coat*, dark blue cloth, double breasted, with rolling collar, black astrachan fur on collar, breast, and cuff, braid same as regimental frock-coat. To be worn as an overcoat with scarlet scarf or muffler. *Cap:* black astrachan fur, 4 inches deep in front and 5 inches behind. To be worn with ear-flaps in cold weather. *Boots:* Canadian. To be worn over the trousers, and to reach the knee. *Gauntlets:* black astrachan. (Kane's List.)

1864. *May* 4.—Orderly Officers to wear cocked hat with feather.

December 22.—Frock-coats abolished for all Officers except Regimental Colonels. Patrol jacket approved for Officers, blue beaver, edged all round with mohair braid, and traced inside with soft roundback loops up front, with four rows of olivettes, crow-toe pockets, trimmed side seams, with Austrian knot below and the Russian braid tree at top. Russian braid tree in centre of back at bottom. Austrian knot on sleeves, with 1-inch braid inside, 9 inches deep. Stand and fall collar, with hook and eye; 1-inch braid all round on both sides. (Kane's List.)

1865. *February* 4.—Gold-laced booted overalls to be discontinued. (Kane's List.)

1867. *February* 4.—N.P. forage-cap for rank and file, height 2¾ inches, band 1 inch.

DRIVER OF FIELD ARTILLERY, 1864.

April 1.—Alteration in Officers' patrol jacket. Up open slits at sides, three rows of olivettes, no braid tree on back. No distinctions for rank on jacket. (Kane's List.)

1868. *April* 21.—Officers of the R.A. employed on Staff of the Army to wear same dress as Officers on the General Staff, but Artillery Officers on Regimental Staff will continue to wear the blue tunic. (Kane's List.)

1869. *November* 3.—Tab introduced, in lieu of leather stock. (Kane's List.)

1870. *October* 1.—Patent cork helmet for Officers in India. Officers of horse and field batteries to wear a gilt spike and chin-strap of same pattern as General Staff. (Kane's List.)

1871. *April* 1.—Waterproof cloak for Officers.

December 20.—N.P. forage-cap for staff-sergeants and sergeants, blue cloth; circumference of crown, 1½ inch less than lower edge; gold-wire lace band 1¼ inch wide for staff-sergeants, and 1 inch for sergeants, black leather binding below band; crown of cap to be of eight pieces of cloth, and gold-lace button. Rank and file blue cloth, 3 inches high, top and bottom same size, yellow worsted braid 1 inch wide, and yellow button in centre of crown. (Kane's List.)

1872. *January* 1.—Pantaloons and high boots in lieu of booted overalls and Wellingtons, for mounted Officers.

February 1.—N.P. mess waistcoat and jacket for Officers. (Kane's List.)

1873. *November* 25.—Infantry ankle boot for Garrison Brigades and dismounted men of Field Artillery. Pantaloons and knee-boots for non-commissioned officers and men. (Kane's List.)

1875. *August* 1.—Foot-straps discontinued for non-commissioned officers and men of Garrison Artillery and Coast Brigade; also for dismounted Officers, except at mess, *levées*, drawing-rooms, and in review order. (Kane's List.)

1876. *January* 1.—Colonels commanding districts to wear cocked hat and plume, and, in undress, an embroidered peak to forage-cap. *N.P. stable jacket for Officers:* blue cloth, with scarlet collar and pointed scarlet cuffs, laced all round with gold lace, small gold tracing on collar seam, deep gold twisted cord with small button on each shoulder, to fasten with hooks and eyes, small gilt studs up front, and scarlet lining. A small silver embroidered grenade to be worn, by all ranks, on each side of front of collar upon the red cloth. *Mess waistcoat* for Horse Brigades: scarlet cloth, with collar, ½-in. gold lace all round, including collar, row of gold Russian braid to form eyes down the front, with figures; pockets edged with gold Russian tracing braid, crow's feet, with figure 8 at each end, and crow's feet in centre. To fasten with hooks and eyes, and gilt studs up front. The same for Officers of Field and Garrison Artillery and Coast Brigade, excepting the gold Russian braid to form eyes down the front. (Kane's List.)

1877. *December* 1.—N.P. forage-cap for staff-sergeants and sergeants, 2½ inches high, gold lace band 1⅜ inch, and gold wire buttons. Leather binding round bottom discontinued. (Kane's List.)

1878. *April* 1.—N.P. patrol jacket for Field and Garrison Brigades, to replace stable jacket.

May 1.—Cork helmet for Officers of Garrison and Field Artillery, covered with blue cloth, with gilt spike. (Kane's List.)

VICTORIA.

1879. *December* 27.—Brass numerals to be worn on tunic and patrol jacket. (Kane's List.)

1880. *March* 1.—Brass grenades to be worn on collar of tunics and patrol jackets.

November 1.—Officers to wear shoulder-strap of plaited gold Russian braid (to be gold wire cord, *vide* G.O., August 1, 1881), lined with blue, with a small button. Badges of rank to be worn on shoulder-straps instead of on collars. (Kane's List.)

1881. *August* 1.—Grenade of frosted silver to be worn at each end of the collar of the dress jacket of Officers of R.H.A., and the tunic of Officers of R.A. A gilt ball and cup to be worn on helmet, in lieu of spike. (Kane's List.)

1882. *October* 1.—Embroidered titles of territorial divisions to be worn on shoulder-strap of Garrison Artillery, in lieu of brass numerals. A crow's foot to be worn by sergeant-majors R.H.A., on sleeves of stable jacket.

December 1.—Grenades and numerals not to be worn on the great-coat. (Kane's List.)

1883. *March* 1.—N.P. forage-cap (oval in shape) for warrant officers, non-commissioned officers, and men. (Kane's List.)

ROYAL ARTILLERY.

GENERAL AND STAFF OFFICERS.

1883. *May* 17. *General Officers.*—The uniform and horse furniture prescribed for their rank.

Officers on the General Staff, or on the Personal Staff of General Officers.—The uniform and horse furniture prescribed for their respective appointments, in every particular.

Officers on the Staff of the Royal Artillery.[*]—Uniform, dress and undress, and horse furniture, in every respect as for Officers holding similar appointments on the General Staff, except that the tunic and jacket are blue with scarlet cloth collar and cuffs, the sword-knot, cloak, and cape of regimental pattern, the shoulder-straps, the lace on the tunic, and that of the dress trousers, the forage-cap, and the belts, and the scarlet stripes of the undress pantaloons and trousers, are of Artillery pattern and width. The full-dress

---

[*] General Officers on the Staff of the Royal Artillery wear the blue tunic with scarlet cuffs, but in all other respects as for General Staff of their rank.

Royal Artillery pouch-belt and pouch will be worn in both dress and undress uniform. The peak to forage-cap will be the same as that for the General Staff both as regards shape and embroidery. The sabretasche for mounted duties will be that described for Staff Officers at page 6,* but with slings of Artillery pattern. *Aides-de-Camp to Inspectors-General of Royal Artillery, and General Officers of Artillery holding Artillery Commands,* wear the belts laid down for Aides-de-Camp to General Officers and Governors at page 31.*

Colonels on the Staff of the Royal Artillery, Colonels commanding Royal Artillery Districts and Regimental Colonels, in full dress wear regimental uniform with cocked hat and plume; when mounted in review order, gold-laced pantaloons and steel spurs. In undress, as detailed above for Staff of the Royal Artillery. In mess dress, regimental uniform. Horse furniture as prescribed for Colonels on the Staff at page 17.* The regimental sword and scabbard are worn in all orders of dress.

Colonels on the Staff of the Royal Artillery, Colonels commanding Royal Artillery Districts, and Regimental Colonels who may belong to the Royal Horse Artillery, wear, in full dress, regimental uniform and horse furniture, and in undress as laid down in preceding para.

NOTE.—Officers commanding Auxiliary Artillery wear regimental uniform, and in full dress a cocked hat and plume, as for an Assistant Adjutant-General.

HORSE BRIGADES AND RIDING ESTABLISHMENT.

Full Dress.

Jacket.—Blue cloth, edged all round with gold cord, forming a figure 8 at the bottom of each back seam. Scarlet cloth collar, edged all round with gold cord; laced as described below, according to rank; and with a grenade embroidered in frosted silver $2\frac{3}{4}$ inches long at each end of the collar. On each side in front, loops of gold cord, $1\frac{3}{8}$ inch apart from centre to centre, fastening with ball buttons, and a crow's foot at the top of the loops. Gold cord along the back seams, forming a crow's foot at the top of each seam, and an Austrian knot at each side of the waist. Shoulder-straps of plaited gold wire cord, lined with blue, a small button of regimental pattern at the top. Badges of rank embroidered in silver.

Field Officers have $\frac{5}{8}$-inch lace all round the collar, within the cord; and a chevron

* "Dress Regulations for the Army." 1883.

VICTORIA.

of 1½-inch lace on each cuff, with figured braiding above and below the lace, extending to 11 inches from the bottom of the cuff.

Captains and Lieutenants have lace round the top only of the collar; and an Austrian knot of gold cord on each sleeve, 7 inches deep, traced round with gold braid 8 inches deep and figured for Captains, 7½ inches deep and plain for Lieutenants.

Lace.—Gold, of regimental pattern.

Buttons.—Gilt, burnished, with a gun and crown.

Trousers, etc.—Blue cloth, with 1¾-inch lace down the side seams; Wellington boots, and brass spurs.

Pantaloons, etc., for Mounted Duties.—Blue cloth, with scarlet stripes 1¾ inch wide down seams; knee boots and steel spurs, as described at page 1,* except that there is a V cut at the top in front of the knee boots.

Busby.—Black sable skin, 7½ inches high in front, 8¾ inches at the back, and 23 inches round the top, outside. A scarlet cloth bag, covering the top of the cap, and falling down the right side to within an inch of the bottom. A spring socket at the top in front. Black leather chin-strap and brass buckle.

Helmet.—White (see pages 4 and 5).*

Cap-line.—Gold cord, with an acorn at each end, passing round the cap diagonally three times, then round the neck, and looped on the left breast.

Plume.—White egret feathers, 9 inches high, with gilt ring and socket.

Sword.—Half-basket steel hilt, with two fluted bars on the outside; black fish-skin grip, bound with silver wire; slightly curved blade, 35½ inches long and 1¼ inch wide, grooved and spear-pointed.

Scabbard.—Steel, with a large shoe at the bottom, and a trumpet-shaped mouth.

Sword-knot.—Gold cord, with a gold acorn.

Sword-belt.—Gold lace, an inch wide, lined with blue Morocco leather; sword-slings of the same width without swivels, and tasche-slings ¾ inch wide; gilt S hook fastening, with "Ubique" on the hook, and two oval gilt plates bearing the Royal Crest.

Sabretasche.—Blue Morocco leather, faced with blue cloth; 1½-inch lace round the face, ¼ inch from the edge. An embroidered device within the lace of the Royal Arms above, and a gun below, with an oak and laurel wreath, and the motto "Ubique" above the gun, and "Quo fas et gloria ducunt" below it.

Pouch.—Blue Morocco leather collapsing pouch, with two pockets; the leaf 5⅝ inches

---

* "Dress Regulations for the Army." 1883.

long and 2¾ inches deep, covered with blue cloth, and edged with ¾-inch lace. An embroidered device within the lace, similar to that on the sabretasche.

Pouch-belt.—Gold lace 2 inches wide, lined with blue Morocco leather; gilt ornamented buckle and slide, and a grenade encircled with a wreath at the end.

Undress.

Patrol Jacket for Officers under the Rank of Regimental Colonel.—Blue cloth, rounded in front, and edged with inch black mohair braid all round and up the openings at the sides; five loops of flat plait on each side in front, fastening with netted olivets, and with crow's feet and olivets at the ends. Stand-and-fall collar. The sleeves ornamented with flat plait, forming crow's feet, 6 inches from the bottom of the cuff. Double flat plait on each back seam, with crow's foot at top and bottom, and two eyes at equal distances. Pockets edged with flat plait, forming crow's feet and eyes. Shoulder-straps, of the same material as the garment, edged with ½-inch black mohair braid, except at the base; black netted button at the top. Badges of rank in gilt metal.

The jacket to be long enough to reach the saddle when the officer is mounted, and loose enough to be worn over the stable jacket.

The patrol jacket is to be worn over, or with a false collar of the same pattern as, the stable jacket.

Trousers.—Blue cloth, with scarlet stripes 1¾ inch wide down the side seams, Wellington boots, and steel spurs.

Pantaloons, etc., for Mounted Duties.—As for full dress.

Forage-cap.—Blue cloth, with band of 1⅜-inch gold lace, gold button and braided figure of special pattern, on the crown. The cap is to be 2⅝ inches high.

Forage-cap for Active Service and Peace Manœuvres.—Blue cloth folding cap, 4½ inches high, with blue side flaps 4 inches deep, to turn down when required. Gold French braid welts on cap and flaps, and at front and back seams. A grenade embroidered in gold in front.

Stable Jacket.—Blue cloth, with scarlet collar and pointed scarlet cuffs, laced all round, including top of collar, with ¾-inch gold lace, regimental pattern, forming a bull's eye at the bottom of each back seam; small gold tracing on collar seam; hooks and eyes down the front, a row of small gilt studs on the left side, scarlet lining. Shoulder-straps with badges of rank as for tunic.

Field Officers have a flat chevron of inch lace, extending to 6 inches from the bottom of the cuff, with braided eyes above and below the lace, the bottom of the braiding to reach just over the top of the scarlet cuff.

Captains have on each sleeve an Austrian knot of ¼-inch gold Russia braid, traced with ⅛-inch braid. A further tracing of eyes above and below the knot. The Austrian knot extends to 7½ inches from the bottom of the sleeve, the figured braiding to 8 inches.

Lieutenants: as for Captains, but without the tracing of eyes.

A silver embroidered grenade to be worn on the collar, as laid down for the dress jacket, but only 1¾ inch long.

Mess Waistcoat.—Scarlet cloth with collar; ½-inch gold lace, regimental pattern, all round, including collar; row of gold Russia braid to form eyes down the front, inside the lace, with figures according to pattern; pockets edged with gold Russia tracing braid, forming a crow's foot and eye at each end, and crow's feet in centre. To fasten with hooks and eyes; small gilt studs up front.

Kamarband.—See page 6.*

Sword-belt.—Black patent leather, 1⅛ inch wide, with mountings similar to those of the dress belt.

Sword-knot.—As for full dress.

Sabretasche.—Black patent leather, with regimental badge, in gilt metal.

Pouch.—Black patent leather collapsing pouch, with two pockets 5¾ inches long, 2⅜ inches deep. A gun in gilt metal on the leaf.

Pouch-belt and other Articles.—As in full dress.

Cloak.—Blue cloth, with sleeves. Stand-and-fall collar, with three black hooks and eyes in front, and three small flat silk buttons at the bottom to fasten the cape. Round loose cuffs, 6 inches deep. A pocket in each side seam outside, and one in the left breast inside. Four buttons down the front. A cloth back strap, to fasten with a large flat silk button at the top of each pocket; a similar button in front on the right to hold the end of the back strap when it is not buttoned across behind. White shalloon lining. The cloak to reach within 8 inches of the ground. Shoulder-straps of the same material as the garment; a small button of regimental pattern at the top. Badges of rank in gilt metal.

Cape.—Blue cloth, 32 inches deep, lined with white shalloon. A cloth band round the top, to fasten with a cloth strap and black buckle; and a fly inside the band, with three button-holes for attaching cape to cloak. Three buttons down the front.

* "Dress Regulations for the Army." 1883.

Regimental Staff Officers.

The same uniform as for the other Officers of their respective honorary or relative rank.

Horse Furniture.

Shabracque.—Blue cloth, 47 inches long at the bottom, and 30 inches deep; rounded before and behind, with 2-inch gold lace and a Vandyked border of scarlet cloth round the edges; a gun, with the Royal Cypher and crown above, and the motto "Ubique" below it, embroidered in gold, at each hind corner.

The other articles as described for Cavalry Regiments.*

FIELD AND GARRISON ARTILLERY, AND COAST BRIGADE.

Full Dress.

Tunic.—Blue cloth, with scarlet cloth collar; the collar and sleeves laced and braided according to rank, with a grenade at each end of the collar, as detailed for Horse Brigades; the skirt rounded in front, closed behind, with a plait at each side, and lined with black; buttons down the front, $2\frac{1}{4}$ inches apart, and two at the waist behind; scarlet cloth edging all round, except the collar, and up the skirt-plaits; shoulder-straps with badges of rank as laid down for Horse Brigades.

Helmet.—Home pattern (see page 4).*

Helmet-plate.—Gilt device: the Royal Arms with gun below, "Ubique" above the gun, and "Quo fas et gloria ducunt" below. Dimensions—

From top of crest to bottom of plate, back measurement, $3\frac{7}{8}$ inches.

Extreme horizontal width, back measurement, 3 inches.

Helmet.—White (see pages 4 and 5).*

Sword-belt.—Gold lace $1\frac{1}{2}$ inch wide lined with blue Morocco leather, and with mountings as for Horse Brigades. Sword-slings (and tasche-slings for mounted Officers) fastened to a flat steel bar covered with blue Morocco leather, and attached to the inside of the belt by four flat steel hooks.

Sabretasche and Pantaloons (for mounted Officers only), Pouch, Pouch-belt, Trousers, Sword, Scabbard, and Sword-knot.—As described for Horse Brigades.

---

* "Dress Regulations for the Army." 1883.

VICTORIA.

Undress.

Mess Waistcoat.—Scarlet cloth, edged all round, including collar, with ½-inch gold lace, regimental pattern; pockets edged with gold Russia tracing braid, forming a crow's foot and eye at each end, with crow's feet in centre; to fasten with hooks and eyes, small gilt studs up front.

Sword-belt.—White patent leather, $1\tfrac{7}{10}$ inch wide, with sword-slings and (tasche-slings for mounted Officers) gilt; frosted plate, with regimental device.

Sword-knot.—Buff leather, ½ inch wide, with runner and gold acorn.

Pouch-belt.—White patent leather, 2 inches wide.

Patrol Jacket, Trousers, Pantaloons (for mounted duties), Forage-cap, Forage-cap for Active Service and Peace Manœuvres, Stable Jacket, Kamarband, Sabretasche (for mounted Officers), Pouch, Cloak, and Cape.—As described for Horse Brigades.

Regimental Staff Officers.

The same uniform as the other Officers of their respective honorary or relative rank.

Horse Furniture.

For mounted Officers, as described for Horse Brigades, except that the shabracque and dress lambskin are not worn.

1891.—*Boots.*—Wellington boots and brass spurs; knee boots and steel spurs, as described at page 1,* except that there is a V cut at the top in front of the knee boots.

Boots and Spurs.—Mounted Officers, except where otherwise specified, wear, when on mounted duties, knee boots with jack spurs fastened with straps and buckles; Officers who are not mounted wear Wellington, or ankle, boots. The knee boots must be, as regards shape, in accordance with the sealed pattern, but the height will depend upon the length of the leg and the relative height of the calf. The boot, which is sloped down at the back, should reach in front to about 4 inches from the top of the knee, and at the back just to the top of the calf.

OFFICER R.A., DRILL ORDER STABLE JACKET, 1894.

* "Dress Regulations for the Army." 1891.

Plate XXIII.

A CAPTAIN OF THE ROYAL HORSE ARTILLERY.

1893.

Description of Plate.

In Plate No. VII. was seen the uniform worn on the formation of the first troop of Horse Artillery, "the Chestnut Troop." Here is seen the same troop a century afterwards.

This was the uniform worn at the Queen's Diamond Jubilee, June 22, 1897.

Shabracques were worn on this occasion for the last time.

Authorities.—Studies from life.
Photographs of the period.
Uniform in existence.
"Dress Regulations for the Army." 1883.
"Dress Regulations for the Army." 1891.
"Dress Regulations for the Army." 1894.

VICTORIA.

April 1. *Busby.*—Black sable skin, 6¼ inches high in front, 7¾ inches at the back, and ½ inch smaller round the top than the bottom; a scarlet cloth bag, covering the top of the cap, and falling down the right side to within an inch of the bottom; a spring socket at the top in front; black leather chin-strap and brass buckle.

Plume.—White egret feathers, 13 inches high, with gilt ring and socket.

Serge Patrol-jacket.—Blue serge; welted seams; stand-up collar, square in front, fastened with one hook and eye, a grenade, 2¼ inches long, in gold embroidery, at each end; shoulder-straps of the same material as the garment, fastened at the top with a small black netted button, ½ inch in diameter, badges of rank embroidered in gold; five gilt ball-buttons down the front; a slit on each side; sleeves ornamented with flat plait forming crow's feet, 6 inches from bottom of the cuffs; two inside breast-pockets, and watch-pocket.

FIELD AND GARRISON ARTILLERY, AND COAST BRIGADE.

Full Dress.

Tunic.—Blue cloth, with scarlet cloth collar, square in front, but slightly rounded at the corners; hook and eye at the bottom, black silk tab. The collar and sleeves laced and braided according to rank, with a grenade at each end of the collar, as detailed for Horse Brigades. The skirt square in front, open behind, with a blue cloth flap on back of each skirt; flaps edged with round gold cord, traced inside with gold Russia braid. Skirt lined with black. Scarlet cloth edging down the front, and at the opening behind. Nine buttons down the front, three buttons on each flap behind, and two at the waist behind. Shoulder-straps with badges of rank as laid down for Horse Artillery.

Binocular-case.—Black patent leather, to hold a binocular field glass, solid leather flap; a gun in gilt metal on the flap.

Sword-belt and Sword-knot (Undress).—White buff leather, $1\frac{7}{10}$ inch wide, with sword-slings (and tasche-slings for mounted Officers), gilt, frosted plate with regimental device; knot, of buff leather, ½ inch wide, with runner and gold acorn.

Pouch-belt.—White buff leather, 2 inches wide.

HORSE ARTILLERY AND RIDING ESTABLISHMENT.

Horse Furniture.

Shabracque.—Blue cloth, 47 inches long at the bottom, and 30 inches deep, rounded before and behind, with 2-inch gold lace and a Vandyked border of scarlet cloth round

Plate XXIV.

A CAPTAIN OF GARRISON ARTILLERY, AND A LIEUTENANT OF FIELD ARTILLERY.

1897.

Description of Plate.

The uniform of 1897 has undergone very slight alteration from that worn in Plate XXII., with the exception that helmets and jackboots have been substituted for busbies and booted overalls.

The collars of the tunic have become higher, and the sleeves tighter.

This was the uniform worn at the Diamond Jubilee.

Authorities.—Studies from life.
Photographs of the period.
Uniform in existence.
"Dress Regulations for the Army." 1883.
"Dress Regulations for the Army." 1891.
"Dress Regulations for the Army." 1894.

VICTORIA.

the edges, a gun, with the Royal Cypher and crown above, and the motto "Ubique" below it, embroidered in gold, at each hind corner. The other articles as described for Cavalry Regiments.

Shabracques and dress and undress lambskins are not worn in India.

Saddle.—Hussar pattern, with brass head and cantle; stirrups according to sealed pattern; blue girths; brown leather wallets.

Bridle.—Brown leather, with brass whole buckles; bent branch bit, with pads and plain bent bar; link-and-tee bridoon; plain leather head-collar; bit-head and bridoon rein sewn on; bosses on bit and ear bosses, of authorized regimental patterns.

Chain.—Steel, with swivel, rings, and spring hook.

Breast-plate and Crupper.—Brown leather, with brass whole buckles and bosses as on bit.

Surcingle and Shabracque Strap.—Brown leather.

Dress Lambskin.—Black Ukraine lambskin, 3 feet 6 inches long and 13 inches deep, edged with scarlet cloth, and lined with moleskin. Not worn in India.

Undress Lambskin.—Black Ukraine lambskin, with black leather seat and large flap to open for wallets, edged and lined as the dress lambskin. Not worn in India.*

OFFICER R.A., MESS DRESS, 1891.

DRIVER FIELD ARTILLERY, 1895.

1894. *April* 1. *Serge Patrol Jacket.*—Blue; full in the chest; collar, cuffs, and shoulder-straps of same colour and material as the rest of the jacket; stand-up collar, square in front, fastened with two hooks and eyes, with grenades $2\frac{1}{4}$ inches long, in gold embroidery; shoulder-straps fastened at the top with small regimental button, badges of rank embroidered in gold; three regimental gilt ball buttons down the front; four pleats at the waist behind, and two pleats at each side in front; a band round the waist, with regimental gilt ball button, to fasten in front; a patch pocket with flap and

---

* "Dress Regulations for the Army." 1891.

small regimental button on each breast; a patch pocket with flap on each side below the band; pointed cuffs, 4½ inches deep, with hole and small regimental button; small pleat each side of point.

CORPORAL R.A. (FIELD),
1897.

GUNNER R.H.A.,
1897.

GUNNER R.A. (GARRISON),
1897.

Forage-cap for Active Service and Peace Manœuvres.—Blue cloth folding cap, 4½ inches high, with blue side flaps, 3½ inches deep, to turn down when required. Gold French braid welts on cap and flaps, and at front and back seams. Embroidered badge on the left side; a grenade in gold, with a scroll under it bearing the motto "Ubique" in silver, on a scarlet ground.

FIELD AND GARRISON ARTILLERY.

Horse Furniture.

For mounted Officers, as described for Horse Artillery, except that the shabracque and dress lambskin are not worn.

Undress lambskins are not worn in India.

Headrope.—Pattern, "Rope, head, cotton," page 69, Vocabulary of Stores.*

1894-1897. Stable jackets for Officers of the Horse, Field, and Garrison

PATROL JACKET, 1897.

SERGE PATROL JACKET, 1897.

Artillery have been abolished, and the serge patrol jacket as described above taken into wear instead.

1897. Shabracques for Officers of the Royal Horse Artillery have now been abolished.

* "Dress Regulations for the Army." 1894.

ERRATA.

LIST OF ORIGINAL GUARANTORS AND SUBSCRIBERS.

Page 122, Jones, T. J., *for* capt. *read* col.
„ 122, Josselyn, J. E., *for* capt. *read* col.
„ 123, Rideout, H. K., *for* H. K. *read* A. K.
„ 123, Rooke, H. W., *for* capt. *read* col.
„ 129, Rothe, G. W. C., *for* capt. *read* col.

LIST OF ORIGINAL GUARANTORS AND SUBSCRIBERS.

GUARANTORS.

Abdy, A. J., maj.
Acland, F. E. D., capt.
Addington, *Hon*. H. W., capt.
Alderson, *Sir* H. J., maj.-gen.
Alexander, R., maj.-gen.
Alexander, W. P., capt.
Alleyne, *Sir* J., maj.-gen.
Anderson, R. D., capt.
Annand, J. H., col.
Arderne, D. D., lieut.
Askwith, H. F., capt.
Askwith, Mrs. W. H.
Baker, A. S., capt.
Baker, E. M., lieut.-col.
Balfour, W. E. L., maj.
Barker, J. S. S., lieut.-col.
Barlow, G. N. H., maj.
Bateman, B. M., capt.
Berkley, J., capt.
Beynon, H. L. N., capt.
Birch, J. F. N., capt.
Blackley, J. H., col.
Blaksley, E., col.
Bland-Hunt, E. S. de V., lieut.
Blane, C. F., maj.
Blewitt, C. T., maj.
Blewitt, W. E., maj.
Blunt, E. W., maj.
Bowles, F. A., lieut.-col.
Brady, R. M , maj.
Breakey, A. J., capt.
Browell, E. T., col.

Browning, H. S., lieut.
Brownlow, H. B., capt.
Burgmann, G. J., col.
Burnett, *Sir* T., *Bart.*, col.
Burney, P. de S., capt.
Burton, H., maj.
Burton, Mrs. A.
Campbell, E. A., capt.
Campbell, M. S. C., capt.
Cantlie, W. H. N., 2nd lieut.
Carey, W., col.
Carroll, A. L., maj.
Carte, T. E., maj.
Carter, A. H., maj.
Casey, C. L., lieut.-col.
Challenor, C. R., lieut.-col.
Chapman, L. J. A., lieut.-col.
Cleeve, W. F., maj.
Cockburn, W. F., maj.
Cooper, E. S., capt.
Cooper, F. E., maj.
Cooper, P. T., capt.
Costobadie, H. H., lieut.-col.
Crampton, F. H., maj.
Craufurd, H. R. G., lieut.
Crookenden, H. H., col.
Crozier, T. H., capt.
Cummings, W. H., maj.
Cunningham, Mrs. J. D.
Dalrymple, F. B., maj.
Dalton, J. C., col.
Davies, E. W., capt.

LIST OF ORIGINAL GUARANTORS AND SUBSCRIBERS.

Dean-Pitt, D. C., maj.
Denne, A. B., capt.
Denne, L. H., maj.-gen.
de Rougemont, C. H., capt.
Desborough, A. P. H., capt.
de Smidt, E. M., 2nd lieut.
Dickinson, Mrs. T. M.
Ditmas, F. F., col.
Dodgson, H. B., capt.
Downes, L., lieut.-col.
Eden, W. A., col.
Ellershaw, A., lieut.
Ellershaw, W., lieut.
Elliot, E. H., maj.
Ellis, C. H. F., col.
Ellissen, G. E., lieut.
Empson, C. A., lieut.-col.
England, A. E., lieut.-col.
Enthoven, P. H., maj.
Ferrar, H. M., capt.
Ferrier, A W., lieut.-col.
Fleming, E. W., lieut.-col.
Forestier-Walker, G. T., capt.
Forster, B. L., lieut.-gen.
Foster, J. R., maj.
Foster, R. C., maj.
Gardiner, S., lieut.-col.
Gascoigne, F. R. T., maj.
Geoghegan, R., capt.
Gillespie, J. C., col.
Gillman, W., lieut.
Gloag, A. R., lieut.-gen.
Goodenough, *Lady* W. H.
Goodeve, H. H., col.
Goodson, F., 2nd lieut.
Grierson, J. M., lieut.-col.
Griffin, H. L., capt.
Groves, J. Percy, lieut.-col.
Guille, H. S. le M., capt.
Hadaway, G. R., lieut.-col.
Hall, E. F., capt.
Hall, F. H., lieut.-col.
Hammond, P. H., lieut.-col.
Hanna, W., maj.
Hansard, A. C., maj.
Hanwell, J., capt.
Harness, A , maj.-gen.

Harrison, R. A. G., maj.
Hay, J., lieut.
Hay-Coghlan, P. H., 2nd lieut.
Haymes, R. L., lieut.
Headlam, J. E. W., capt.
Heffernan, N. B., capt.
Henry, J., lieut.
Hibbert, A. L., maj.
Hickman, H. P., maj.
Hill, H. B., lieut.
Hopkins, M. O., maj.
Horton, S. G., capt.
Hozier, H. M., V.D., col.
Hume, C. V., lieut.-col.
Hunt, H. V., lieut.-col.
Hutchinson, W. L., lieut.-col.
Inglefield, N. B., maj.
Jervis, W. N., col.
Jocelyn, J. R. J., lieut.-col.
Johnstone, H., lieut.
Jones, T. J., capt.
Josselyn, J. E., capt.
Kelaart, G. T., maj.
Kenyon, L. R., capt.
Kilner, C. H., capt.
Kingscote, H. B., col.
Lamb, G. R., capt.
Lamont, J. W. F., lieut
Leach, R. P., maj.
Le Cocq, H., gen.
Leslie, J. H., maj.
Lewes, H. C., maj.-gen.
Lloyd, F. T., maj.-gen.
Lloyd, M. B., capt.
Lockhart, R. D. E., col.
Lyall, C. N., capt.
Lyall, H., maj.
Lyon, C., capt.
Maberly, C. E., maj.
Macdonald, A. D., Esq.
Macdonald, Mrs.
Macdonald, R. J., capt.
Macdonald, *Hon.* W. J.
McDonnell, J., lieut.-col.
Macgregor, P. L., col.
Macintyre, J. M'K , lieut.-gen.
McKay, D., capt.

LIST OF ORIGINAL GUARANTORS AND SUBSCRIBERS.

Mackenzie, C. G., capt.
Mackenzie-Grieve, J. A., maj.
Mackintosh, J. B., lieut.
MacMunn, G. F., lieut.
Magenis, H. C., maj.-gen.
Maitland, R. P., capt.
Manifold, J. F., maj.
Markham, *Sir* E., lieut.-gen.
Marshall, G. H., maj.-gen.
Maule, H. B., maj.-gen.
Maunsell, M. C., capt.
Maxwell, J. McC., capt.
May, E. S., maj.
Milman, G. H. L., maj.-gen.
Montanaro, A. F., maj.
Montgomery, R. A., col.
Montgomery, R. A. K., capt.
Morley, C., col.
Morrieson, H. W., maj.
Murdoch, W. W., col.
Murray, J., Esq.
Murray, J. M., col.
Nairne, *Sir* C. E., lieut.-gen.
Nelson, H. S., maj.
Newton, J. W. M., maj.
Nicholson, S. J., maj.-gen.
Nicolls, O. H. A., maj.-gen.
Norris, E. E., capt.
Nutt, A. C. R., lieut.
Ogilvie, N. S., maj.
Oldfield, A. R., lieut.
Ollivant, E. A., col.
O'Malley, G. H., col.
Ormiston, J. W., capt.
Owen, C. H. W., lieut.
Owen, C. R. B., lieut.
Owen, J. F., maj.-gen.
Paget, V. F. W. A., capt.
Paget, W. L. H., maj.
Palmer, H. R., capt.
Paterson, E. H., maj.
Phillipps-Treby, P. W., maj.-gen.
Plant, W. A., maj.
Pollard-Urquhart, F. E. R., lieut.-col.
Pollock, E., maj.
Poole, F. C., lieut.
Pottinger, E. C., capt.

Powell, H. L., capt.
Pretyman, G. T., maj.-gen.
Purvis, A. B., maj.
Ramsden, H., lieut.
Reid, H. A., capt.
Reid, J. W., capt.
Richardson, J. B., maj.-gen.
Rideout, H. K., maj.-gen.
Roberts, *Rt. Hon.* F. S. *Lord*, field mar.
Rooke, H. W., capt.
Rowe, O., maj.
Ryan, E. H., lieut.-col.
Saltren-Willett, A. J., capt.
Sandars, E. C., lieut.
Sandes, H. T. T., col.
Sandilands, P. H., maj.-gen.
Sandys, W. B. R., capt.
Saunders, A. A., brig.-gen.
Savile, W. C., maj.
Scott, C. E. S., col.
Seton, A. D., maj.
Seton, A. M., 2nd lieut.
Shakerley, H. W., col.
Shea, H. J. F., col.
Shore, *Hon.* F. W. J., lieut.-col.
Simpson, W. H. R., maj.-gen.
Slade, F. G., col.
Slade, J. R., col.
Smeaton, C. O., capt.
Smith, H. G., capt.
Smith, W. H. U., lieut.
Smyth, *Sir* H. A., gen.
Soames, H., capt.
Spender, W. B., 2nd lieut.
Spring, F. W. M., col.
Stephenson, K., maj.
Stevens, C. F., capt.
Stewart, A. A., maj.-gen.
Stewart, R. Macg., maj.-gen.
Stirling, J. S., col.
Stokes, A., maj.
Stone, F. G., maj.
Strange, H. B., capt.
Stratton, J. H., col.
Swann, C. J. H., lieut.
Swinton, Arthur, lieut.-col.
Theobald, C. P., lieut.-col.

LIST OF ORIGINAL GUARANTORS AND SUBSCRIBERS.

Thrupp, F. M., capt.
Thurn and Taxis, *H.S.H. Prince* Eric of.
Torriano, C. E., col.
Trench, C. C., col.
Turner, A. E., col.
Turner-Emery, H., col.
Vallentin, H. E., lieut.
Vane-stow, H., maj.
Vaughan-Hughes, E., maj.
Vigne, R. A., capt.
Vincent, H. O., capt.
Wailes, W. E., lieut.
Walford, N. L., col.
Waller, W. N., maj.-gen.
Ward, F. H., maj.
Ward, W., col.

Warden, R. E., capt.
Watkins, L. G., maj.
Watson, W. H., col.
Weir, H. G., lieut.-col.
White, W. L., maj.
White-Thomson, H. D., capt.
Williams, A. H. W., maj.-gen.
Williams, M. S., capt.
Williams, W. H., maj.
Wilson, *Sir* Alex., *Bart.*
Wray, J. C., capt.
Wylde, R. D., lieut.
Yorke, F. A., lieut.-col.
Young, J. E. H., lieut.
Younger, J., col.
Officers' Mess, Meerut.

SUBSCRIBERS.

Abdy, A. J., maj.
Acland, F. E. D., capt.
Acton, T. H. E., maj.
Aikenhead, F., capt.
Aikman, J., surg. lieut.-col.
Aitken, W., col.
Aldershot Military Society.
Alexander, G. D'A., maj.
Alexander, J. H., col.
Allcard, H., 2nd lieut.
Allen, E. G., Esq.
Anderson, E. B., maj.
Anderson, J. D., capt.
Anley, W. B., lieut.
Anstruther-Duncan, A. W., col.
Appleyard, G. C., lieut.
Arbuthnot, G., col.
Armitage, W. T., lieut.
Arnold, W. R., lieut.
Arthy, W., capt.
Askwith, J. B. H., capt.
Atchison, C. H., lieut.-col.
Atlay, H. W., lieut.

Aylmer, F. A., lieut.-col.
Bailward, A. C., maj.
Bainbridge, E., col.
Baker, G. D., maj.
Baker, R. H. S., lieut.-col.
Baldwin, J. G., capt.
Balguy, J. H., maj.
Banister, F. M., lieut.-col.
Barron, H., col.
Barry, J. D., capt.
Barton, P., lieut.
Barton, R. L., lieut.
Baylay, F. G., col.
Bayley, G. H. W., lieut.
Beatson, W. J. A., maj.
Beaver, F. T. M., lieut.-col.
Becke, A. F., lieut.
Bedford, His Grace *the Duke of*.
Bedwell, E. P., 2nd lieut.
Begbie, A. R. G., lieut.
Bell, M. D., lieut.
Bell-Irving, A., maj.
Benson, G. E., maj.

LIST OF ORIGINAL GUARANTORS AND SUBSCRIBERS.

Benson, R. P., capt.
Best, G., lieut.-col.
Betty, J. F., col.
Biddulph, M., lieut.
Biddulph, Sir R., gen.
Bigg, F., maj.
Bigge, Sir A. J., lieut.-col.
Bignell, B. H., 2nd lieut.
Birch, A. C., lieut.
Birch, E. M., lieut.
Birch, F. H. J., maj.
Bird, M. H. C., 2nd lieut.
Birtwistle, A., 2nd lieut.
Bishop, C. F., lieut.
Blackwood, P. F., maj.
Blandy, W. P., lieut.-col.
Block, M. W. P., maj.
Blount, C. H., maj.
Blunt, C. H., maj.-gen.
Boileau, A. C. T., maj.
Bond, H. H., lieut.
Bond, R. F. X. M'G., capt.
Bonham-Carter, Miss M. G.
Boothby, G. M., capt.
Bouwens, L. H., lieut.-col.
Brendon, A., maj.-gen.
Briscoe, A. V., maj.
Broadrick, F. B. D., capt.
Brock, H. J., lieut.
Brough, J. F., col.
Brown, F. T., lieut.
Browne, H. R. Y., lieut.-col.
Bruce-Kingsmill, J. C. de K., capt.
Buckle, E., lieut.-col.
Budworth, C. E. D., lieut.
Bullen, S. D., lieut.
Bunbury, W. St. P., maj.
Bunny, F. B., lieut.-col.
Burne, E. R., 2nd lieut.
Burnett, J. C., capt.
Burrard, W. D., capt.
Burt, J. M., maj.
Butcher, A. E. A., maj.
Butler, Sir W., maj.-gen.
Buzzard, C. N., lieut.
Buzzard, T., Esq., M.D.
Cadell, H. E., capt.

Cadell, J. F., capt.
Calvert, A. M., col.
Cambier, E. F., col.
Cameron, E. C., capt.
Cameron, R. B. M., lieut.
Campbell, A. N., 2nd lieut.
Campbell, Herbert M., capt.
Campbell, P. J., maj.-gen.
Campbell-Johnston, G., capt.
Capel-Cure, A., capt.
Carbutt, E. G., lieut.
Cardew, G. A., capt.
Carey, F. W., col.
Carey, G. V., 2nd lieut.
Carey, W. D., maj.-gen.
Cartwright, G. N., capt.
Casement, R., capt.
Castens, W. E., lieut.
Caulfield, C. T., capt.
Cayley, A. M., lieut.
Chamberlain, T. ff., maj.
Chamberlin, A. B., maj.
Chamier, G. D., maj.
Chapman, E. F., gen.
Chepmell, C. H., capt.
Chevalley, F., lieut.
Christie, L. B. S., lieut.
Clapham, D., 2nd lieut.
Clark, C. W., capt.
Clarke, G. V., lieut.
Clarke, H. C. S., lieut.
Clarke, Sir A., lieut.-gen. R.E.
Clarke, Sir G. S., lieut.-col. R.E.
Clayton, E., col.
Clayton, G. F., 2nd lieut.
Clayton, Mrs. R.
Climo, P. H., 2nd lieut.
Cloete, E. R. H. J., capt.
Close, H. M., 2nd lieut.
Coates, R. C., lieut.
Coker, L. E., lieut.-col.
Colclough, G., maj.-gen.
Coley-Bromfield, J. C., capt.
Combe, K., capt.
Connal, A. C., capt.
Coode, H. P. R., lieut.
Cookson, J. G., gen.

Corbyn, H., capt.
Cotton, W., lieut.-col.
Cotton-Jodrell, E. T. D., capt.
Courtenay, M. H., capt.
Coxhead, J. A., lieut.-col.
Craig, J. F., maj.
Crawford, A., capt.
Crockett, S. L., lieut.
Crockett, W. M., capt
Crowe, J. H. V., capt.
Cunliffe, F. L., maj.
Currie, A. C., capt.
Curteis, F. A., maj.
Curzon, W. S., col.
Dallas, J. H. L., maj.
Dames, T. L., capt.
Daniell, A. C., maj.
Daniell, de C., col.
Daniells, J., and Co.
Darley, G. R., maj.
Davidson, F. M., capt.
Davidson, W. L., lieut.-col.
Davson, H. M., lieut.
Dawkins, H. S., maj.
Dawkins, J. W. G., capt.
Dawson, H. F., lieut.
Dawson-Scott, G. N., lieut.
Day, R., Esq., J.P.
de Berry, G. J. L., capt.
de Jersey, W. G., maj.
Denne, A. B., capt.
Dennis, J. B., maj.-gen.
Dent, F. W., lieut.
De Prée, H. D., lieut.
Deshon, F. G. T., 2nd lieut.
Despard, W. H. C., lieut.
Dickinson, Mrs. T. M.
Disney, T. R., col.
Dixon, E. T., lieut.
Dixon, M. C., maj.-gen.
Douglas, J. S., maj.
Downes, M. F., maj.-gen.
Drake, B. F., capt.
Drake, H. M., lieut.
Du Boulay, E. de V., capt.
Du Cane, H. J., maj.
Duff, W. S., capt.

Dunlop, A. S., capt.
Dunlop, J. W., maj.
Dunnage, A. J., col.
Du Plat, Sir C. T., maj.-gen.
Du Plat-Taylor, St. J. L. H., capt.
Duthie, W. H. M., lieut.-col.
Dwyer, G. T. C., lieut.
Dyson, L. M., lieut.
Dyson-Perrins, C. W., Esq.
Eaton-Evans, H. J., lieut.
Eden, W. R., lieut.
Edgar, J. S., lieut.
Edlmann, E. E., lieut.
Edmeades, H., maj.-gen.
Edwards, A. C., lieut.
Elles, *Sir* E. R., brig.-gen.
Ellington, E. L., 2nd lieut.
Elliot, H. M., capt.
Elton, F. A. G. Y., capt.
Emery, W. B., lieut.
England, E. P., capt.
England, R., lieut.
Farmar, W. L., capt.
Fasson, D. J. M., capt.
Fawcett, P. H., capt.
Fawcus, H., 2nd lieut.
Fell, J. P., maj.
Fendall, C. P., maj.
Findlay, N. D., maj.
Finlay, R. F., 2nd lieut.
Firth, B. A., Esq.
Fisher, F. T., capt.
Fitz Gibbon, J. A., lieut.
Fitz Maurice, R., capt.
Fitz Roy, E. A., lieut.-col.
Fitzroy, P. Fitz W., lieut.
Forbes, A., lieut.
Forde, L., maj.
Fordyce-Buchan, G. C., capt.
Forestier-Walker, C. E., capt.
Forster, Mrs. E.
Forsyth, J. A. C., 2nd lieut.
Fortescue, *Hon.* J. W.
Foster, P. L., lieut.
Fowler, W. J., lieut.-col.
Fox, A. M., 2nd lieut.
Free, J. F., col.

LIST OF ORIGINAL GUARANTORS AND SUBSCRIBERS.

Freeth, J. P., lieut.-col.
Frith, W. H., lieut.-col.
Fulton, J. B. D., 2nd lieut.
Furnivall, W., 2nd lieut.
Furze, E. W., 2nd lieut.
Galbraith, G. E., capt.
Galpin, T. D., Esq.
Garnett-Botfield, W. D., maj.
Garrett, E., lieut.-col.
Gascoigne, F. R. T., maj.
Gayer, H. W., 2nd lieut.
Geary, H., maj.
Geary, H. Le G., maj.-gen.
Gethin, R. W., St. L., 2nd lieut.
Godfray, H. C. W., lieut.
Godfrey-Faussett, P. G., capt.
Goff, A. H. S., capt.
Goldie, A. H., lieut.
Goold-Adams, H. E. F., maj.
Gordon, A. W. B., maj.
Gordon, L. G. F., capt.
Gorham, C. A., col.
Græme, F. J., maj.
Graham, W. F., lieut.-col.
Graham-Clarke, L. A., capt.
Gray, M. Mc N., lieut.
Grayson, A. D. H., lieut.
Greenhill, A. G., Esq.
Grevel, H., and Co.
Grimston, W. J., maj.
Grylls, J. B., 2nd lieut.
Guinness, C. D., maj.
Guinness, E., maj.
Guise, H., maj.
Gunner, E., maj.
Hadcock, A. G., lieut.
Hadden, C. F., lieut.-col.
Haig, A. G., 2nd lieut.
Hale, E. T., lieut.
Hall, Mrs. F. E.
Hankey, J. C. G. A., lieut.
Hanna, J. C., lieut.
Hanwell, J., maj.-gen.
Harding-Newman, E., lieut.
Hardy, W. K., capt.
Hare, R. H., capt.
Harman, Mrs., J. F.

Harpur, E. H., lieut.
Hawkes, C. St. L. G., lieut.
Hawkshaw, E. C., maj.
Hawkshaw, J. C., Esq.
Hay, E. O., col.
Hay, Malcolm, Esq.
Haynes, K. E., lieut.
Henning, P. W. B., lieut.
Henry, G. C., col.
Henshaw, C. G., capt.
Henvey, R., lieut.
Hervey, C. R. W., lieut.-col.
Heyman, C. E. H., maj.
Hickie, A. F., capt.
Hill, *Sir* E. S., col.
Hill, R. R., 2nd lieut.
Hill, R. T., lieut.
Hills-Johnes, Sir J., lieut.-gen.
Hine-Haycock, V. R., lieut.
Hodgins, C. R., capt.
Hogg, R. E. T., 2nd lieut.
Holdsworth, J. K., col.
Holland, C. S., 2nd lieut.
Holland, E. C. F., maj.
Hollinshead, H. N. B., lieut.
Honner, W. J., maj.
Hooper, S. H., capt.
Horne, H. S., maj.
Hoste, D. E., maj.-gen.
Hotham, J., lieut.-col.
Howard-Vyse, C., lieut.
Hoyle, J. R., Esq.
Hudson, T. R. C., capt.
Hughes, A. J., maj.
Hume, C. V., lieut.-col.
Humphreys, G., capt.
Hunt, W. H., lieut.
Hutchinson, C. H., capt.
Hutchinson, F. P., capt.
Hutchinson, W. F. M., maj.-gen.
Hutchison, K. D., 2nd lieut.
Hutton, H., lieut.-col.
Iles, H. W., capt.
Innes, H. M., lieut.
Irving, L. H., Esq.
Jackson, H. K., maj.
Jackson, L. D., capt.

LIST OF ORIGINAL GUARANTORS AND SUBSCRIBERS.

Jackson, M. B. G., maj.
Jacob, A. L. B., lieut.
James, W. R. W., maj.
Jameson, W. K. E., 2nd lieut.
Jeffreys, H. B., maj.
Jellett, J. H., maj.
Jennison, H. G. W., lieut.
Jervis-White-Jervis, *Sir* J. H., *Bart.*, maj.
Jeudwine, H. S., capt.
Johnson, R. M., lieut.
Johnston, J. H. B., lieut.
Johnston, J. T., maj.
Jones, W. H., capt.
Julian, C. J., 2nd lieut.
Kane, A. H., lieut.
Keir, J. L., maj.
Kelly, R. M. B. F., maj.
Kemble, W. E., lieut.
Kemmis, W., col.
Kempson, J. W., lieut.
Kennedy, A. C., lieut.
Kensington, E., col.
Kent, F. E., maj.
Kerrison, E. R. A., maj.
Keys, G., Batty. sergt.-maj.
Keyworth, R. G., lieut.
King, A. H., maj.-gen.
King-Harman, W. H., col.
Kingscote, H. B., col.
Kirk, J. C., capt.
Kirke, H. L., capt.
Kirkpatrick, A. R. Y., lieut.
Knight, C. L. W. M., capt.
Knox, A. R., capt.
Knox, W. G., col.
Kough, T. M., lieut.
Labalmondiere, J. A., maj.
Lacey, T., lieut.
Laird, G., capt.
Lake, H. A., capt.
Lamb, G. R., capt.
Lambert, T., capt.
Lane, C. W. M., maj.
Langley, J. P., maj.
Langley, W. S., col.
Langston, D., master gun.
Lardner-Clarke, J. de W., maj.

Lawrie, C. E., maj.
Leader, H. P., capt.
Leahy, H. G., capt.
Lecky, F. B., maj.
Lecky, R. St. C., capt.
Lennard, *Sir* J. F., *Bart.*, capt.
Levita, C. B., capt.
Lewin, H. F. E., lieut.
Lewis, G., lieut.
Livingstone-Learmonth, J. E. C., 2nd lieut.
Livingstone-Learmonth, L. C., lieut.
Lockyer, W. N., col.
Long, C. W., lieut.-col.
Loraine, F. E. B., lieut.-col.
Lowe, F. M., maj.
Lushington, S., capt.
Lynes, S. P., col.
Macdonald, A. D., Esq.
Macdonald, J. C., Miss
Macdonald, W. B., lieut. R.N.
Macdonald, *The Hon.* W. J.
MacDougall, J. P., 2nd lieut.
McLaughlin, G. H., maj.
McLeod, R. G., M'Q., maj.
McMeekan, F. H. F. R., capt.
McMicking, G., capt.
Maidlow, J. S., lieut.
Malet, G. E. W., maj.
Manger, H. E., capt.
Manley, W. G. H., lieut.
Mansell, J. H., capt.
Marshall, G. H., maj.-gen.
Marshall, H. C., capt.
Marton, R. O., lieut.
Masson, C. G., maj.
Maunsell, F. R., capt.
Mercer, H. F., maj.
Metcalfe, F. H., lieut.
Metcalfe, S. F., lieut.
Milner-Gibson-Gillum, G., Esq.
Montgomery, R. A. K., capt.
Moore, St. L. M., capt.
Moore, W. H., lieut.
Morgan, F. C., lieut.-col.
Morris, Mowbray, Esq.
Mulliken, C. F. L., lieut.
Mundy, R. E., col.

LIST OF ORIGINAL GUARANTORS AND SUBSCRIBERS.

Musgrave, A. D., lieut.
Myers, A. E. C., lieut.
Neal, G., lieut.
Ness, P., Esq.
Nevinson, T., St. A. B. L., lieut.
Newbigging, P. C. E., lieut.-col.
Newcome, H. W., lieut.
Nichol, W. D., capt.
Nicholson, G. H. W., capt.
Nicolls, E. G., maj.
Nixon-Eckersall, F. E., lieut.
Noble, *Sir* A., capt.
Normand, S. R., lieut.
Norris, A. G., capt.
Oakes, R., maj.
O'Kinealy, J., lieut.
Oldfield, A. R., lieut.
Oldfield, H. E., maj.
Oldfield, R., maj.-gen.
Olivier, W. H., capt.
Ollivant, E. A., col.
O'Malley, C. L., lieut.
O'Neill, W. H., maj.
Onslow, W. H., capt.
Orr, C. W. J., lieut.
Otter-Barry, F. M., 2nd lieut.
Ouseley, R. G., capt.
Owen, C. C., capt.
Owen, C. H., maj.-gen.
Palmer, C. C., lieut.
Palmer, H. R., capt.
Parry, J. B., capt.
Parsons, E. H. T., capt.
Parsons, L. W., lieut.-col.
Partridge, R. G., lieut.
Peake, M., capt.
Perceval, E. M., maj.
Perrott, T., lieut.-col.
Phelips, H. P. P., capt.
Phillipps, C., capt.
Phillips, E. H., 2nd lieut.
Phillpotts, A. H. C., maj.
Phipps, C. E., capt.
Pickwoad, E. H., maj.
Pitman, A. C., capt.
Playfair, G. J., *Lord*, lieut.-col.
Pollard-Urquhart, F. E. R., lieut.-col.

Popplestone, W. H., capt.
Porteous, J. J., maj.
Potts, J. W. H., lieut.-col.
Prendergast, F., cap.
Preston, D'A. B., maj.
Pringle, G. O. S., capt.
Quain, J., lieut.
Radcliff, F. W., maj.
Radcliffe, R. E. L., capt.
Rainsford-Hannay, R. W., col.
Rait, A. J., lieut.-col.
Ramsay, *Hon.* C. M., lieut.
Ramsden, R. E., 2nd lieut.
Reade, P. N. G., lieut.
Reid, J. W., capt.
Rettie, W. J. K., capt.
Rice, G. W., capt.
Rich, C. C., lieut.-col.
Riddell, E. V. D., lieut.
Rigg, R. A., maj.
Ritchie, J., lieut.-col.
Robertson, J. A., maj.
Robson, W., lieut.
Rochford-Boyd, H. C., 2nd lieut.
Ropes, J. C., Esq.
Ross-Johnson, C. M., capt.
Rothe, G. W. C., capt.
Ruck-Keene, R. F., lieut.
Rugge-Price, C. F., capt.
Rundle, G. R. T., maj.
Rundle, H. M. L., maj.-gen.
Russell, C., lieut.-col.
Russell, E. S. E. W., lieut.
Ryan, C. A., maj.
Sandilands, P. H., maj.-gen.
Sargeaunt, H. G., lieut.
Saunders, W. P., capt.
Saunders-Knox-Gore, W. A. G., maj.
Schofield, A., Esq., M.D.
Schofield, H. N., capt.
Schofield, Miss.
Schreiber, C. B., lieut.
Sclater, H. C., maj.
Scott, A. B., capt.
Scott, A. F. S., capt.
Scott, C. W., lieut.
Seddon, E. McM., capt.

LIST OF ORIGINAL GUARANTORS AND SUBSCRIBERS.

Sedgwick, F. R., 2nd lieut.
Sharp, H., Esq.
Sherer, J. D., lieut.
Short, A. H., capt.
Short, W. A., lieut.
Simpson, A. C. S. W., lieut.
Simpson, G. G., maj.
Simpson, H. C. C. D., maj.
Simpson, R. H., lieut.-col.
Skipwith, P. A., lieut.
Slator, G. F., lieut.
Slee, P. H., capt.
Smith, C. M., Esq.
Smith, Edmund P., capt.
Smith, Edward P., capt.
Smith, Granville, capt.
Smith, H. B., lieut.
Smith, L. A., lieut.
Smith, W. W., col.
Smith-Rewse, H. B. W., 2nd lieut.
Spalding, W. B., 2nd lieut.
Spencer, H., lieut.
Spencer, J. W. T., lieut.-col.
Spragge, C. H., brig.-gen.
Stanbrough, L. K., lieut.
Stanley, Hon. G. F., lieut.
Stanton, H. E., maj.
Stapylton, G. J. C., lieut.
Staveley, W. C., capt.
Stevens, G. M., lieut.-col.
Stevenson, R. C., capt.
Stewart, Mrs.
Stewart, W. L., Esq
Stirling, C., lieut.
Stirling, J. W., maj.
Strode, W. W., Esq.
Strong, W., lieut.
Supple, K. L., Esq.
Swettenham, W. A. W., lieut.
Tailyour, G. H. F., 2nd lieut.
Talbot-Ponsonby, E. F., lieut.
Tennant, H. L., capt.
Thomas, C. S. W., 2nd lieut.
Thomas, H. M., lieut.
Thomson, C. W., col.
Thwaites, W., capt.
Toms, F. B. R., maj.

Townshend, G. R., maj.
Tremaine, R., capt.
Trotter, J. K., lieut.-col.
Tupper, G. Le M., lieut.-gen.
Turner, F. M., lieut.-col.
Tyler, A. M., capt.
Tyler, C. W., capt.
Tyler, R. E., capt.
Tyler, T. B., maj.-gen.
Uniacke, H. C. C., capt.
Vandeleur, H. M., 2nd lieut.
Van-Staubenzee, C. C., capt.
Vaughan-Jackson, H., Esq.
Wakefield, T. M., 2nd lieut.
Waldron, F., maj.
Walford, N. L., col.
Walker, A. L., capt.
Walker, E. H., lieut.-col.
Wall, M. D., lieut.
Warburton, W. M., 2nd lieut.
Ward, E., maj.
Ward, H. D. O., lieut.
Ward, M. C. P., capt.
Watkins, C. B., maj.
Watson, J. C., capt.
Watson, S., lieut.-col.
Watts, C. D. R., lieut.
Waymouth, E. G., lieut.
Wemyss, R. E. F., lieut.
Westerman, J. F., lieut.
Wheeler, G. D., lieut.
Whitaker, A. E., capt.
White, G. H. A., lieut.
Wilken, J., maj.
Williams, W. H., maj.
Willis, Sir G., gen.
Wilson, Sir Alex., Bart.
Wilson, C. H., lieut.
Wilson, F. A., lieut.
Wilson, J. R., capt.
Wing, F. D. V., maj.
Wolseley, *The Viscount*, field mar.
Woodifield, A. H., capt.
Woodrow, T. H. J., maj.
Woods, H. C. M., lieut.-col.
Wright, G., maj.
Wynne, H. E. S., 2nd lieut.

LIST OF ORIGINAL GUARANTORS AND SUBSCRIBERS.

Wynter, H. T., lieut.
Yates, H. T. S., lieut.-col.
Young, A. D., capt.
Young, F. H., capt.
Young, H. A., capt.
Young, N. E., maj.
Royal Malta Artillery.
Donegal Artillery.
Edinburgh Artillery.
Glamorgan Artillery.
Guernsey Artillery.
Hants and Isle of Wight Artillery.
Mid-Ulster Artillery.
Northumberland Artillery.
2nd Cinque Ports Volunteer Artillery.
1st Cornwall Volunteer Artillery.
1st Durham Volunteer Artillery.
3rd Durham Volunteer Artillery.
2nd East Riding Yorkshire Volunteer Artillery.
2nd Glamorgan Volunteer Artillery.
1st Gloucester Volunteer Artillery.
1st Lancashire Volunteer Artillery.
3rd Lancashire Volunteer Artillery.
5th Lancashire Volunteer Artillery.
6th Lancashire Volunteer Artillery.
7th Lancashire Volunteer Artillery.
2nd Middlesex Volunteer Artillery.
1st Norfolk Volunteer Artillery.
1st West Riding Yorkshire Volunteer Artillery.

Army and Navy Club.
Junior United Service Club.
Naval and Military Club.
The Charterhouse Library.
The Reference Library, Manchester.
The Royal Engineers Corps Library, Chatham.
The War Office Library.
The Royal Military College Library.
The Men's Library, 16 Co. Eastern Div. R.A.
The Garrison Library, Malta.
The Royal United Service Institution Library.
The Library, No. 6 Mountain Battery R.A.
The Free Public Library, St. John's, New Brunswick.
Officer Commanding 13th Field Battery R.A.
The Officer Commanding 6 Co. Southern Div. R.A.
The Officers, 55th Field Battery R.A.
The Officers' Mess, R.A., Barrackpore.
The Officers' Mess, R.A., Colaba, Bombay.
The Officers' Mess, R.A., Colchester.
The Officers' Mess, R.A. and R.E., Bermuda.
The Officers' Mess, R.A., Cork Harbour.
The Officers' Mess, 46th Field Battery R.A.
The Officers' Mess, No. 6 Mountain Battery R.A.
The Officers' Mess, No. 16 Co. Eastern Div. R.A.
The Officers' Mess, No. 8 Bengal Mountain Battery.
The Officers' Mess, 1st Battn., 5th Regt., Canadian Artillery.
The Royal Artillery Institution.

www.ingramcontent.com/pod-product-compliance
Lightning Source LLC
Chambersburg PA
CBHW081437300426
44108CB00017BA/2389